A World of Birds

by **Vicky Woodgate**

Blueprint
EDITIONS

Contents

Introduction

This book will take you on a flying visit around the world, uncovering some of the finest birds from each of the seven continents. Each bird has been chosen as a representative of its wider family. Some can in fact be found on several continents, while others fly long journeys from one place to another.

Here you will find the most amazing facts about 75 different species and discover the variety and splendor of the bird world. So, are you ready to begin your birding adventure?

A World of Birds

There are over 10,000 species of bird in the world, and they occur in all shapes, sizes, and colors. Some are hunters, preying on fish, mammals, or other birds; some feed on insects and spiders; and some are entirely vegetarian, feeding only on seeds and pollen. But whatever their differences, all birds have a few key features in common.

What is a bird?

Birds are vertebrates, which means they have a hard internal skeleton, just like humans. They all hatch from eggs, and as adults they have beaks, two wings, and feathers covering their bodies. Most birds can fly, but not all of them.

Forehead

Beak or bill

Crown

Nape

Wing

Throat

Rump

Breast

Tail

Flank

Thigh

Leg

Toe

Eurasian jay

Claw

Knowing the proper names for a bird's anatomical parts can be helpful in identifying species.

Dinosaur ancestors

Birds are the descendants of feathered, meat-eating dinosaurs that lived millions of years ago. There are several similarities between dinosaurs and the birds that live today, including their body shapes and some aspects of their lifestyles.

Beaks

The bill, or beak, is an extension of a bird's jaw. It has two parts: the upper and the lower mandible. The shape of a bird's beak is determined by its lifestyle, especially its diet. But beaks can also be useful for preening, nest-building, and even fighting.

Crossbill (below)
This bird's beak has adapted for picking seeds from conifer cones.

Golden eagle (above)
This bird has a sharp, hooked beak for tearing meat off its prey.

Avocet (above)
Avocets use their long bills to find and grab prey hidden underwater in the mud.

Sniff sniff

Like people, birds use their nostrils to breathe, smell, and even to sneeze! Every species except the kiwi has its nostrils located at the top of its beak.

Feet

Most birds have four toes: three facing forward and one at the back. They use them to move about by walking, hopping, or swimming, but they can also use them like hands for building nests or snatching prey.

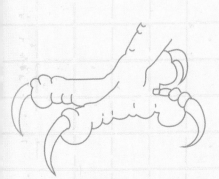

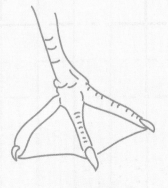

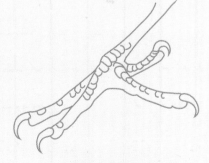

Osprey
This bird of prey has sharp claws called talons.

Sparrow
This little bird has long toes adapted for perching on branches.

Mallard
Webbed feet help this duck swim across the water.

Woodpecker
Two toes at the back help this bird cling vertically onto trees.

Flight

Birds use their strong feathered wings to fly, flapping them up and down to overcome the force of gravity. At the same time, their tails act like the rudder on a boat, controlling their direction and helping them come to a stop—a bit like applying the brakes. Different feather types have different functions during flight, but all combine to give birds a perfectly streamlined shape in the air.

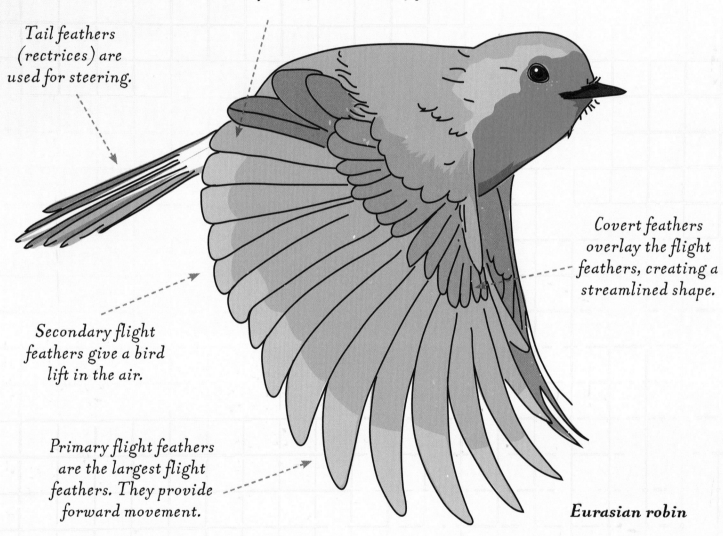

Tertiary flight feathers are less important than primary or secondary feathers.

Tail feathers (rectrices) are used for steering.

Covert feathers overlay the flight feathers, creating a streamlined shape.

Secondary flight feathers give a bird lift in the air.

Primary flight feathers are the largest flight feathers. They provide forward movement.

Eurasian robin

Migration tales

Birds can travel great distances both in search of food and to find mates and breed. Long, seasonal journeys are called migrations and usually occur between winter feeding grounds and summer breeding grounds.

Flight patterns

Wing and tail shapes determine how each species of bird flies. Birds with long, broad wings can easily glide on air currents, while those with smaller, shorter wings are better able to reach fast speeds (see right).

The main part of the feather is called a "vane."

Sprucing up

All birds regularly preen to look after their feathers. They remove dust and dirt, "zip up" individual barbs, and coat their feathers in oil from their preen gland, which keeps them waterproof.

Barbs hook together like velcro.

The central shaft is hollow to keep the feather light.

Fluffy down feathers keep birds warm.

Shed a feather

Adult birds molt at least once a year. This is the process of shedding their old feathers and growing brand new ones.

Feathers

Feathers enable birds to fly, but they also keep birds warm and can be used in bright displays or for camouflage. They are made of a substance called keratin—the same material as human hair and nails—which means they are strong but also light.

Birds such as ducks fly in a fast, straight line.

Finches flap quickly then fold their wings to their sides, giving them a bobbing flight.

Birds of prey glide on air currents, which gives them a spiraling motion.

Eggs

Female birds lay hard-shelled eggs, which is where their young grow into chicks. The egg contains everything a chick needs to grow from a fertilized cell into a tiny bird, ready to hatch out. Once the eggs have been laid, most birds incubate them by sitting on their group of eggs, called a clutch, to keep them warm and safe from harm.

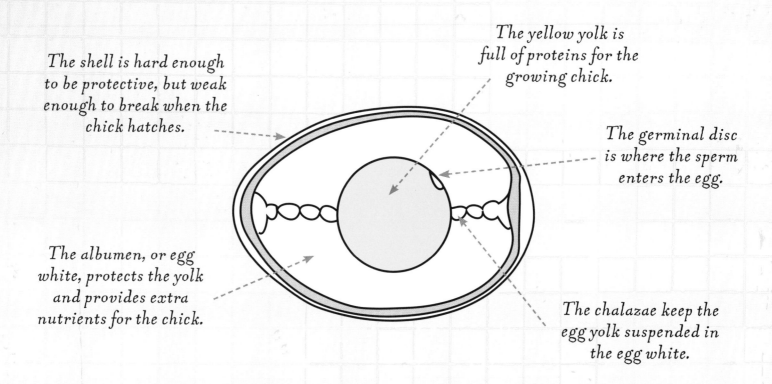

The shell is hard enough to be protective, but weak enough to break when the chick hatches.

The yellow yolk is full of proteins for the growing chick.

The germinal disc is where the sperm enters the egg.

The albumen, or egg white, protects the yolk and provides extra nutrients for the chick.

The chalazae keep the egg yolk suspended in the egg white.

All shapes and sizes

Birds lay eggs in all shapes, sizes, and colors. The largest egg in the world belongs to the ostrich and is nearly 6 inches (15 cm) tall!

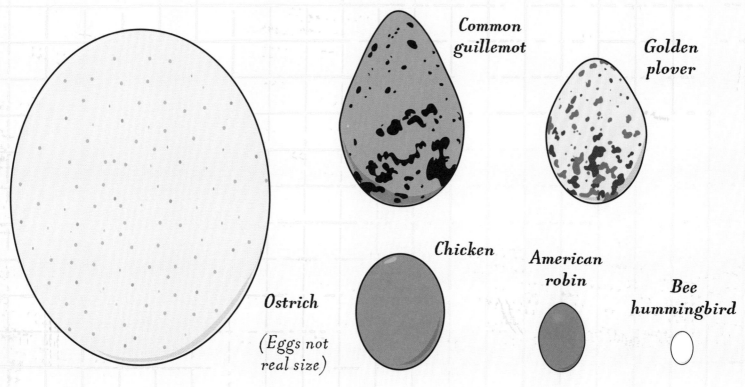

Common guillemot

Golden plover

Chicken

American robin

Bee hummingbird

Ostrich

(Eggs not real size)

Chicks

There are two types of chick. Precocial chicks are fully formed birds, which can stand within minutes, have feathers, and are ready to forage with their parents. Altricial chicks are born helpless. They are bald and blind and need their parents to survive.

Plover
Precocial chick

Hornbill
Altricial chick

Making a nest

Most birds create a nest to hold their eggs. Some are made of a few simple twigs, while others are elaborate structures that can take days or weeks to create. A few birds, such as eagles, return to the same nest every year, gradually making it larger and larger.

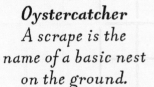

Oystercatcher
A scrape is the name of a basic nest on the ground.

Atlantic puffin
Burrows can be made in cliffs or riverbanks.

American robin
Cup-shaped nests are the most common type of nest.

Little owl
Cavity nests are built inside hollow trees.

Bird families

Birds that form lifelong pair-bonds will be the most attentive of parents. Once hatched, most chicks fight with their siblings to get the greater share of food, and some eagles and boobies even throw their siblings out of the nest. However, in rare instances, birds such as falcons have close sibling bonds and learn by play-fighting together.

Alaska
(USA)

PACIFIC
OCEAN

CANADA

North America

From the North Pole down to the tropics of Central America, this sweeping continent spans frozen plains and hot deserts and includes the hottest place in the world: Death Valley. The birds that live here are as varied as the environments they inhabit. Many species also migrate and there are four major migration routes following coastlines and rivers: the Pacific, Central, Mississippi, and Atlantic flyways. These are used like highways by millions of birds every year.

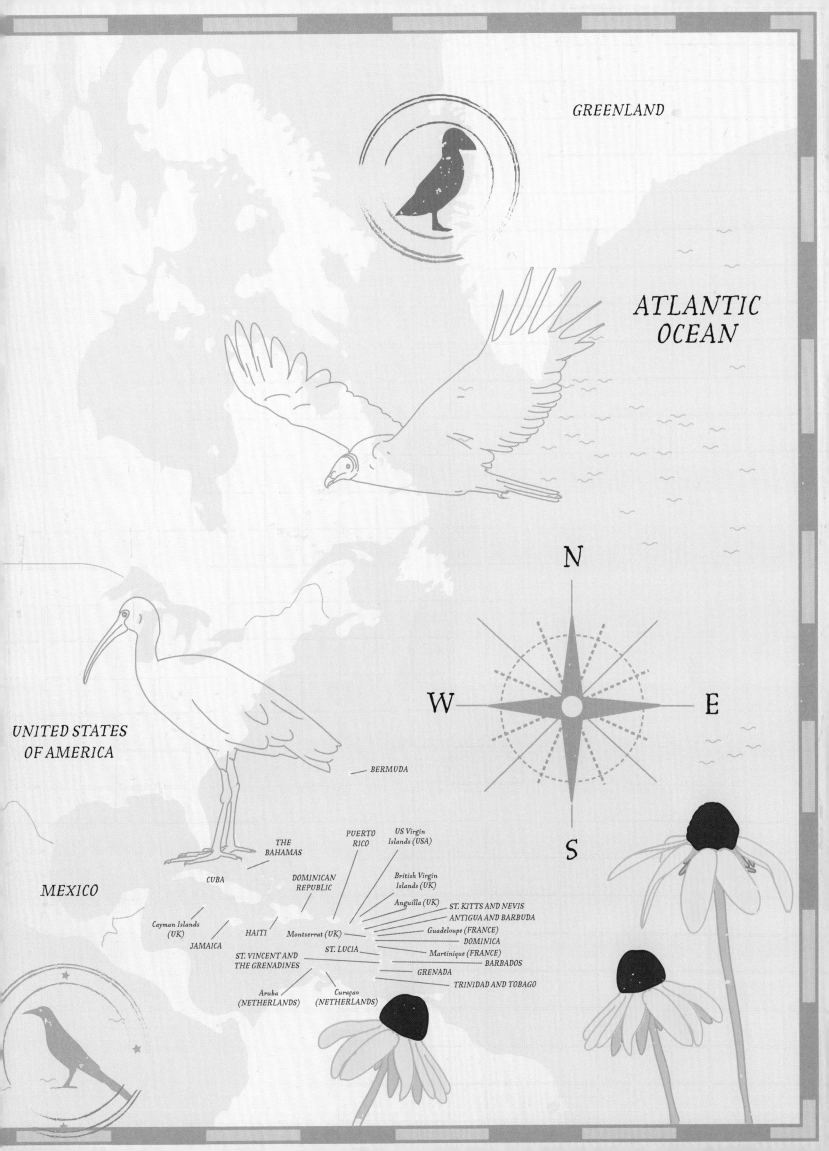

GREENLAND

ATLANTIC
OCEAN

N

W ⊕ E

S

UNITED STATES
OF AMERICA

BERMUDA

MEXICO

CUBA

THE
BAHAMAS

PUERTO
RICO

US Virgin
Islands (USA)

DOMINICAN
REPUBLIC

British Virgin
Islands (UK)

Cayman Islands
(UK)

HAITI

Anguilla (UK)

ST. KITTS AND NEVIS
ANTIGUA AND BARBUDA

JAMAICA

Montserrat (UK)

Guadeloupe (FRANCE)
DOMINICA

ST. VINCENT AND
THE GRENADINES

ST. LUCIA

Martinique (FRANCE)
BARBADOS

GRENADA

Aruba
(NETHERLANDS)

Curaçao
(NETHERLANDS)

TRINIDAD AND TOBAGO

Canada goose
Branta canadensis

This large, rowdy goose is found in North America, Europe, and New Zealand, wherever there is grass to be nibbled. In spring and autumn, flocks undertake long migrations from north to south, flying up to 1,500 miles (2,400 km) in a single day—nearly the width of the Atlantic Ocean. They can be seen snaking through the air in wide V-formations, usually following the same route year after year.

Flocks can fly at up to 40 mph (60 km/h)— easily as fast as a car.

Flying in formation, birds take turns at the front, where they are exposed to stronger currents. When the front bird tires, another takes its place.

KARonk

A male goose is called a gander.

Canada geese can be identified by their white chinstraps.

Males and females look alike.

Not all Canada geese migrate. Some live in the same place year-round, especially near towns.

Goslings

Webbed feet

During breeding season, males can become aggressive and attack anyone that approaches the nest!

Common loon
Gavia immer

The howling wails of the loon can be enough to send shivers down the spine. But unless you are a fish, you have little to fear from this elegant diving bird. Also known as the great northern diver, the loon has a strong, streamlined body, perfectly shaped for slipping through the water. However, it is awkward on land and only steps ashore when nesting.

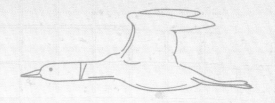

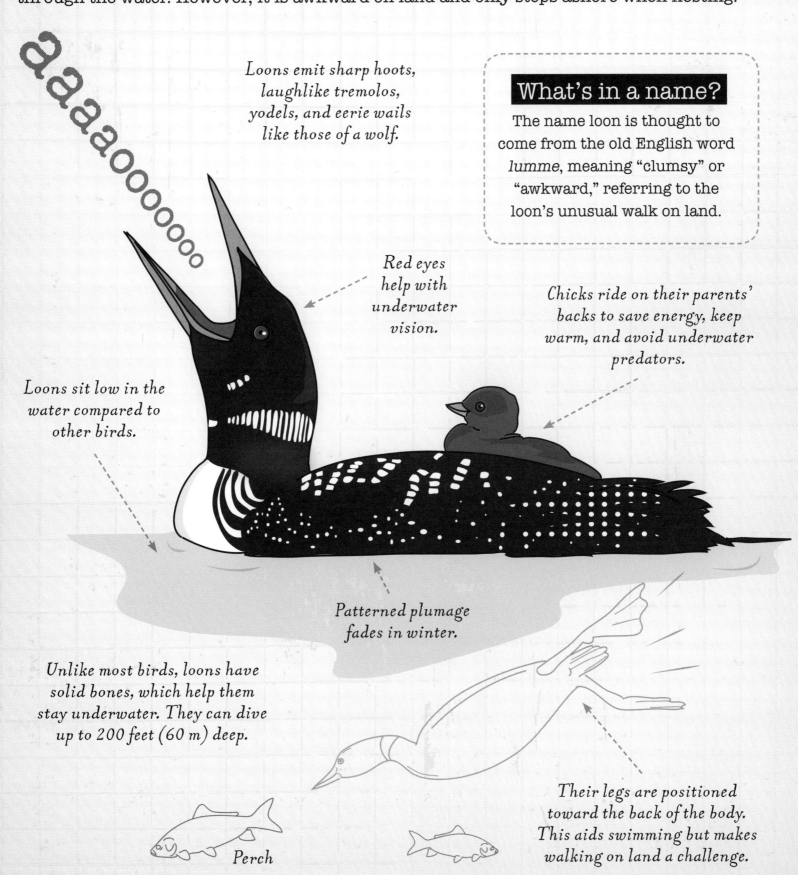

aaaoooooo

Loons emit sharp hoots, laughlike tremolos, yodels, and eerie wails like those of a wolf.

What's in a name?
The name loon is thought to come from the old English word *lumme*, meaning "clumsy" or "awkward," referring to the loon's unusual walk on land.

Red eyes help with underwater vision.

Chicks ride on their parents' backs to save energy, keep warm, and avoid underwater predators.

Loons sit low in the water compared to other birds.

Patterned plumage fades in winter.

Unlike most birds, loons have solid bones, which help them stay underwater. They can dive up to 200 feet (60 m) deep.

Perch

Their legs are positioned toward the back of the body. This aids swimming but makes walking on land a challenge.

15

Wild turkey
Meleagris gallopavo

With their fanned tail display, fleshy wattles, and loud gobbling call, there's no mistaking these all-American birds. But despite their plump, rather ugly appearance, surprisingly turkeys can run as fast as an Olympic sprinter and can change the color of their wattle according to their mood!

Male displaying tail feathers

Unlike domesticated turkeys, wild turkeys can fly short distances, reaching speeds of nearly 55 mph (90 km/h).

The head and wattle turn red to attract a mate or blue if the turkey is afraid.

Males gobble to catch the attention of female turkeys.

gobble gobble

With a top running speed of 25 mph (40 km/h), turkeys are almost as fast as Usain Bolt!

Sharp spur

Turkeys spend the day foraging for acorns, seeds, and snails on the ground, then sleep in trees at night.

Snail

Rock ptarmigan
Lagopus muta

The hardy ptarmigan is a master of camouflage. In summer, its mottled brown plumage is a perfect match with the lichen-covered rocks of the mountains and tundra where it lives. But in winter, its feathers turn pure white to blend in with its snowy surroundings. Even its feet and legs are feathered to help keep it warm in freezing conditions.

Camouflage protects ptarmigans from their natural predators, including Arctic foxes, golden eagles, and weasels.

Ptarmigans are a type of grouse related to pheasants, partridges, and chickens.

Summer plumage

Arctic fox

Red comb

croak croak

Winter plumage

Flocks live together on the ground, feeding on leaves, twigs, and berries.

Feathered legs for warmth

Feathered feet act like snowshoes and stop the birds from sinking into deep snow.

Bald eagle
Haliaeetus leucocephalus

Soaring high over mountains and lakes, these birds of prey are daredevils in the air. Though they mostly feed on fish, they have been known to seize prey as large as raccoons or geese in their razor-sharp talons. Courting birds also perform spectacular acrobatics, falling through the air together and only letting go just before they hit the ground. Once they have mated, they build the largest nest of any bird.

The bird's white head and dark body make it appear bald from a distance.

Courting eagles test each other's strength by locking talons and cartwheeling through the air.

Talons have a grip 10 times stronger than a human's.

Thick, strong legs

6.5 ft (2 m)

Bald eagles add new material to their nest each year. The biggest nest ever found was 8.8 ft (2.7 m) wide and 19 ft (6 m) deep!

Greater roadrunner
Geococcyx californianus

A member of the cuckoo family, this long-legged bird can survive extreme desert conditions, run up to 21 mph (35 km/h), and kill venomous snakes! As its name suggests, it has the habit of running along roads—predominantly because this is a good place to find its main prey, reptiles, which warm themselves on the hot tarmac.

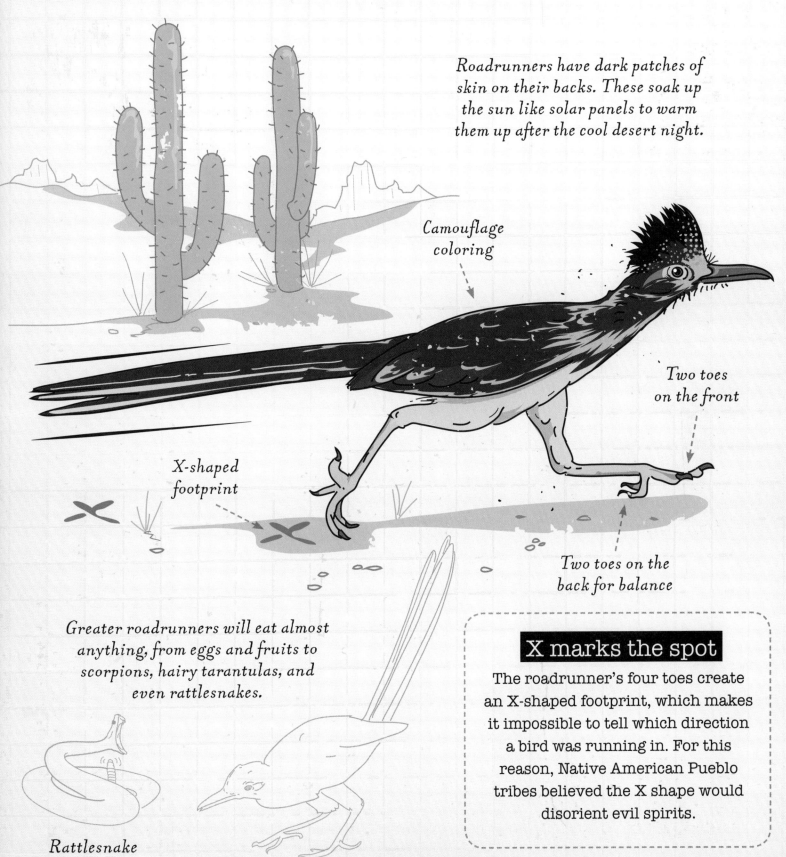

Roadrunners have dark patches of skin on their backs. These soak up the sun like solar panels to warm them up after the cool desert night.

Camouflage coloring

Two toes on the front

X-shaped footprint

Two toes on the back for balance

Greater roadrunners will eat almost anything, from eggs and fruits to scorpions, hairy tarantulas, and even rattlesnakes.

Rattlesnake

X marks the spot

The roadrunner's four toes create an X-shaped footprint, which makes it impossible to tell which direction a bird was running in. For this reason, Native American Pueblo tribes believed the X shape would disorient evil spirits.

Blue jay
Cyanocitta cristata

This pretty blue songbird may look serene, but it shows a feisty side the moment food becomes scarce. Luckily it has a clever trick to deal with this, performing a pitch-perfect impersonation of its top predator, the red-shouldered hawk, in order to scare away its competition.

The crest rises up when the bird is aggressive, excited, or displaying to a mate.

Blue jays will sometimes watch squirrels burying nuts, then go back to steal them later!

Gray squirrel

Strong bill for cracking nuts

Distinctive black collar

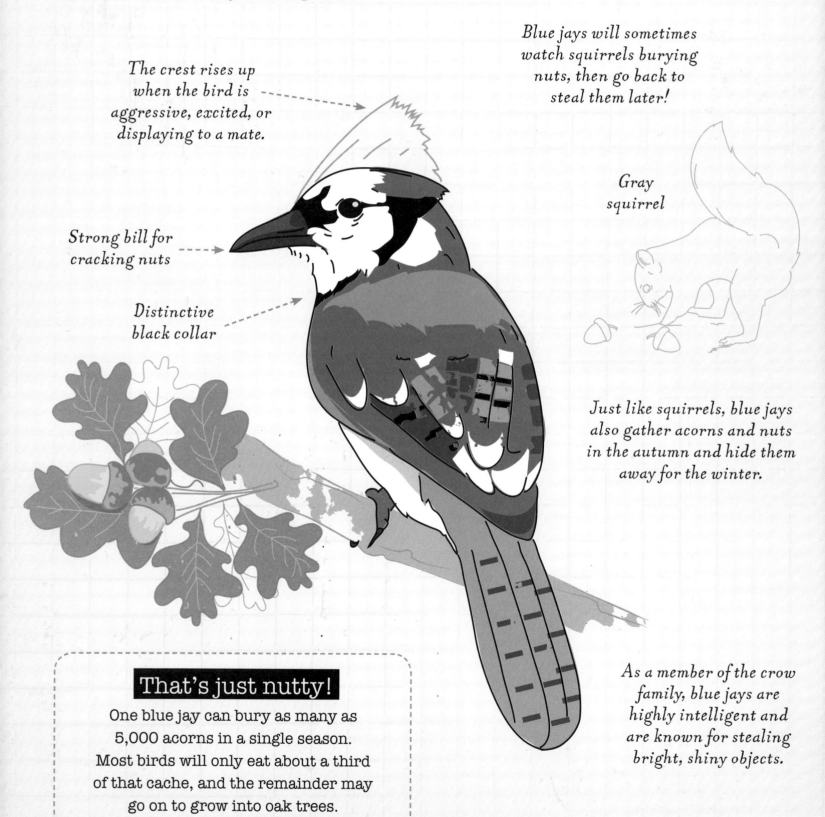

Just like squirrels, blue jays also gather acorns and nuts in the autumn and hide them away for the winter.

That's just nutty!

One blue jay can bury as many as 5,000 acorns in a single season. Most birds will only eat about a third of that cache, and the remainder may go on to grow into oak trees.

As a member of the crow family, blue jays are highly intelligent and are known for stealing bright, shiny objects.

Pileated woodpecker
Dryocopus pileatus

One of the largest woodpeckers in the world, this forest-dweller drills into trees with incredible force, pecking up to 20 times per second as it searches for its favorite food: carpenter ants and beetle larvae that tunnel beneath the bark. Its hard beak carves out neat, rectangular holes and can even snap slender trees in half.

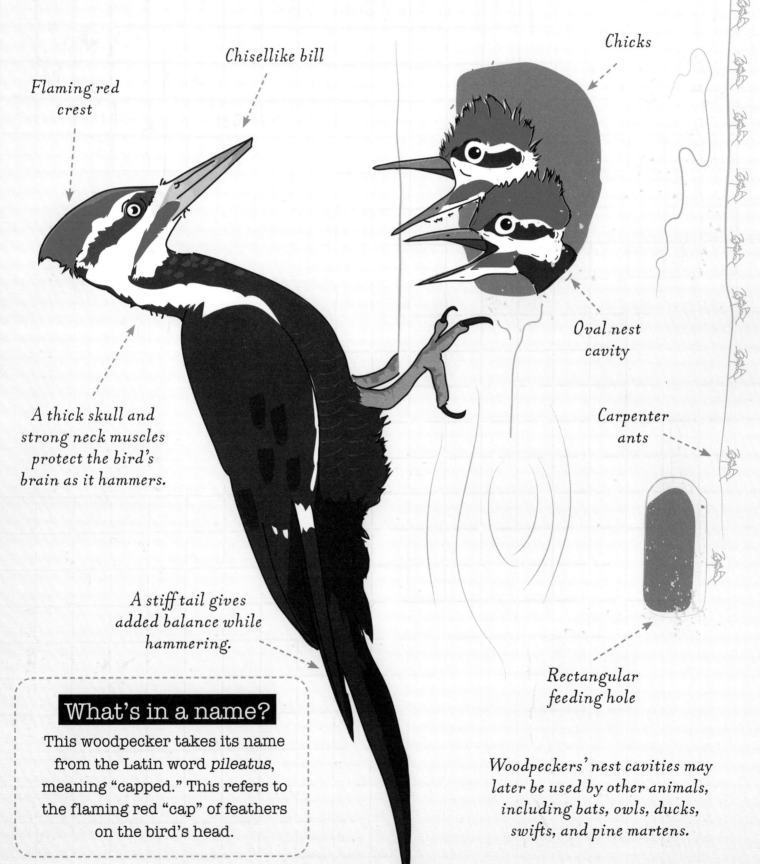

Flaming red crest

Chisellike bill

Chicks

A thick skull and strong neck muscles protect the bird's brain as it hammers.

Oval nest cavity

Carpenter ants

A stiff tail gives added balance while hammering.

Rectangular feeding hole

What's in a name?

This woodpecker takes its name from the Latin word *pileatus*, meaning "capped." This refers to the flaming red "cap" of feathers on the bird's head.

Woodpeckers' nest cavities may later be used by other animals, including bats, owls, ducks, swifts, and pine martens.

American goldfinch

Spinus tristis

The sunshine yellow of the goldfinch is a common sight on garden bird feeders. During summer, males preen and fluff their feathers in front of mousy females before both sexes molt in the autumn and turn olive brown. Careful listeners may hear the birds' flight call, which sounds curiously like "po-ta-to-chip, po-ta-to-chip."

They can often be seen hanging upside down to feed.

In winter, goldfinches may migrate south to Mexico.

Tsee-tsi-tsi-tsit

Stripes of color on the wing are called "wingbars."

Male

Female

Goldfinches mostly feed on seeds, rarely eating anything but a strict vegetarian diet.

Northern cardinal
Cardinalis cardinalis

This bright bird takes its name from the red robes of Catholic priests called cardinals. As it neither migrates nor changes color when it molts, its brilliant feathers can be seen against summer greens or winter snows. Both sexes are fiercely territorial and use their songs to warn away intruders.

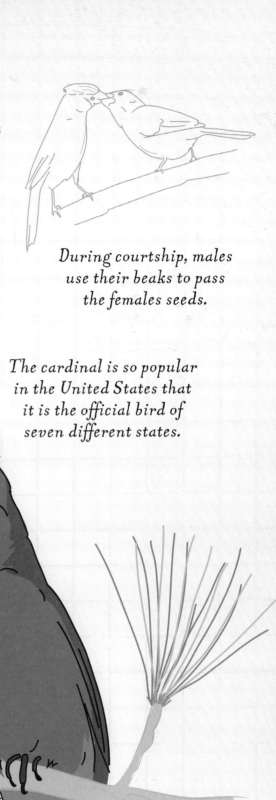

During courtship, males use their beaks to pass the females seeds.

Unlike most songbirds, the female sings from the nest, probably telling the male when to return.

cheer cheer

The cardinal is so popular in the United States that it is the official bird of seven different states.

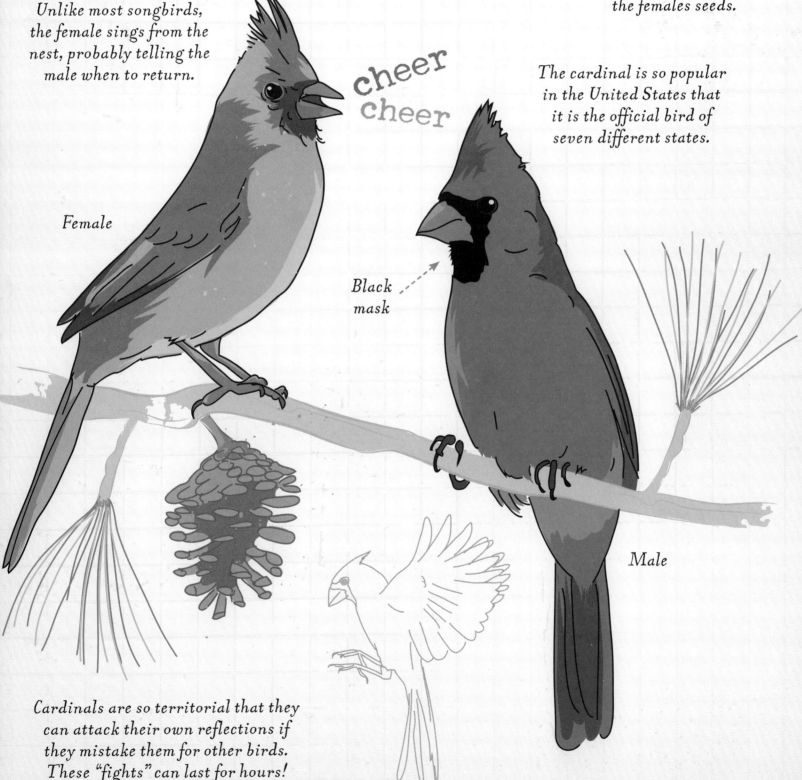

Female

Black mask

Male

Cardinals are so territorial that they can attack their own reflections if they mistake them for other birds. These "fights" can last for hours!

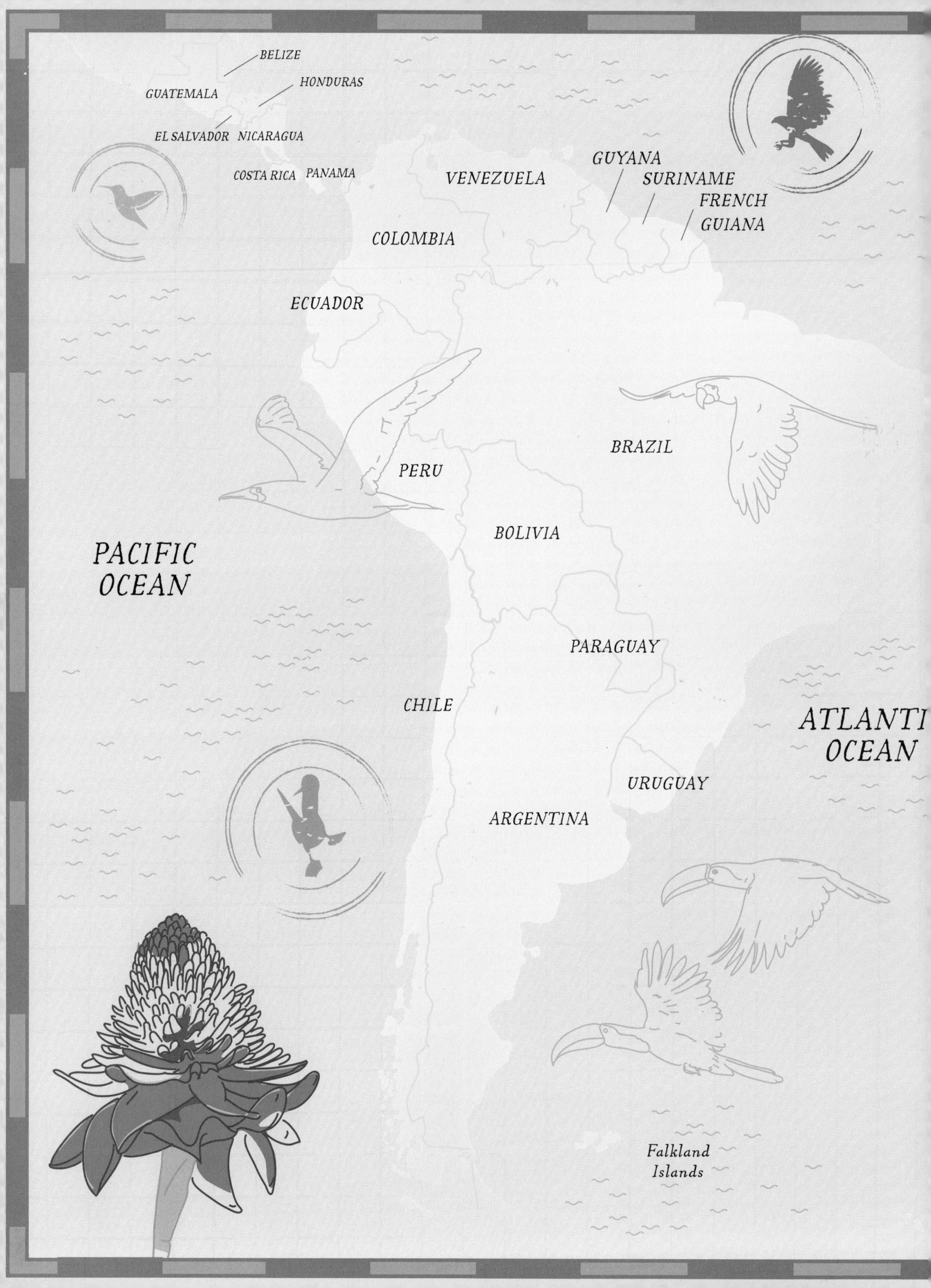

BELIZE

GUATEMALA

HONDURAS

EL SALVADOR   NICARAGUA

COSTA RICA   PANAMA

VENEZUELA

GUYANA

SURINAME

FRENCH
GUIANA

COLOMBIA

ECUADOR

PERU

BRAZIL

BOLIVIA

PACIFIC
OCEAN

PARAGUAY

CHILE

ATLANTI
OCEAN

URUGUAY

ARGENTINA

Falkland
Islands

Central & South America

Stretching from the tropics of Central America toward the waters of Antarctica, South America boasts a huge range of habitats, from rainforests to deserts and snow-topped mountains to rugged coasts. There is such a rich array of birdlife here that species are still being discovered today. Despite vast stretches of untouched wilderness, human development is starting to encroach on these fragile environments, threatening some of the world's most magnificent birds.

N

W — E

S

Greater rhea

Rhea americana

Roaming the sparse grasslands of Central and South America, the rhea is the largest bird on the continent. Despite its large, shaggy wings, it is unable to fly and relies entirely on its long, muscular legs to carry it from danger, running at speeds of over 40 mph (60 km/h). It can also lash out at enemies with a fatal kick!

Nests contain up to 80 eggs from as many as 12 different females.

3.3 ft (1 m)

The flat breastbone lacks a "keel" where flight muscles attach in flying birds.

5 ft (1.5

Bringing up baby

The male rhea is solely responsible for raising his young. Ahead of mating, he prepares a nest, then performs a display to attract females. Several hens will lay their eggs in his nest. The male then incubates the eggs and rears the chicks single-handedly.

Males may sometimes "adopt" stray chicks from another family.

Three-toed feet enable rheas to run faster than most birds (which have four toes).

Featherless legs

Scarlet ibis

Eudocimus ruber

This shocking red wader is one of the brightest birds in the world. It flocks in groups around mangroves, mudflats, and estuaries, using its thin, curved beak to carefully search the mud for crustaceans and other food. In fact, pigments in its shellfish diet give the ibis its vibrant color.

Croak

The long bill is perfectly shaped for probing in the mud.

Usually silent, the ibis grunts and croaks around breeding time.

Ibises fly and forage with other kinds of birds, including spoonbills, egrets, and herons, for safety in numbers.

7.8 in. (20 cm)

Excellent eyesight helps the ibis look for underwater prey.

The bill turns black during breeding season.

Black tips on wings

Ibises feed on a range of aquatic animals, including shrimp, fish, and amphibians.

Mollusk

Shrimp

Fish

Frog

Andean condor

Vultur gryphus

The imposing Andean condor is the largest flying bird in the world. With a body heavier than a car tire, it can only stay in the air thanks to its ten-foot (3 m) wingspan—and even then it relies on air currents to help it glide. Like other vultures, it is a scavenger, scouring the ground for decaying bodies to feed on.

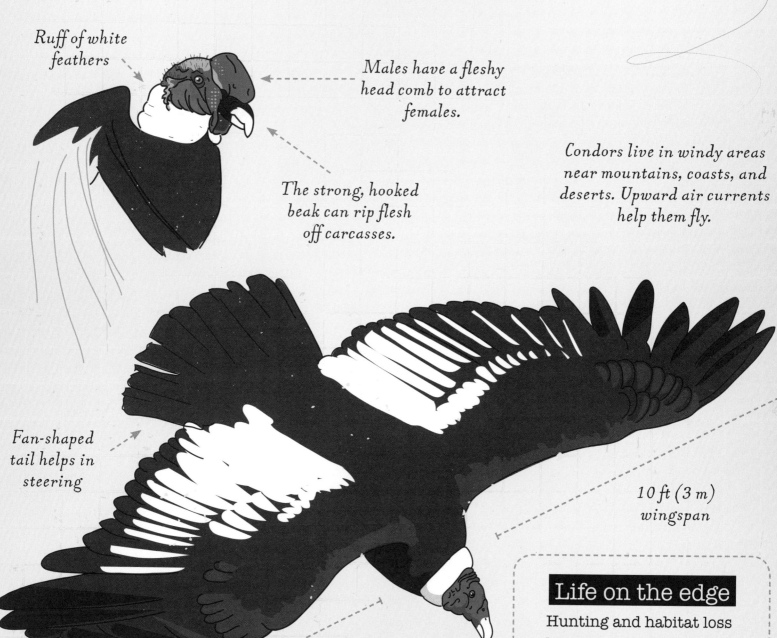

Ruff of white feathers

Males have a fleshy head comb to attract females.

The strong, hooked beak can rip flesh off carcasses.

Condors live in windy areas near mountains, coasts, and deserts. Upward air currents help them fly.

Fan-shaped tail helps in steering

10 ft (3 m) wingspan

Condors play an important ecological cleanup role, feeding on even the largest dead animals—including whales!

Life on the edge

Hunting and habitat loss have drastically reduced the Andean condor's numbers. However, a wave of new efforts means the magnificent condor is slowly making a comeback.

Harpy eagle
Harpia harpyja

With its hooked beak and talons the length of a grizzly bear's claws, the harpy eagle is an impressively large and powerful bird of prey. Perched in the canopy, it searches the rainforest below for signs of movement. Then it dives down on its prey—sometimes snatching monkeys or sloths even larger than itself!

What's in a name?

This eagle is named after the harpies of Greek mythology: winged creatures with the body and claws of an eagle and the face of a beautiful woman.

The harpy can be identified by the crest of feathers around its face.

WHEEEEEEE

This eagle's legs are as thick as a man's wrist, giving it the strength to carry heavy prey.

A small wingspan enables the harpy to weave through dense vegetation.

The harpy's talons are the largest of any bird.

5 in. (13 cm)

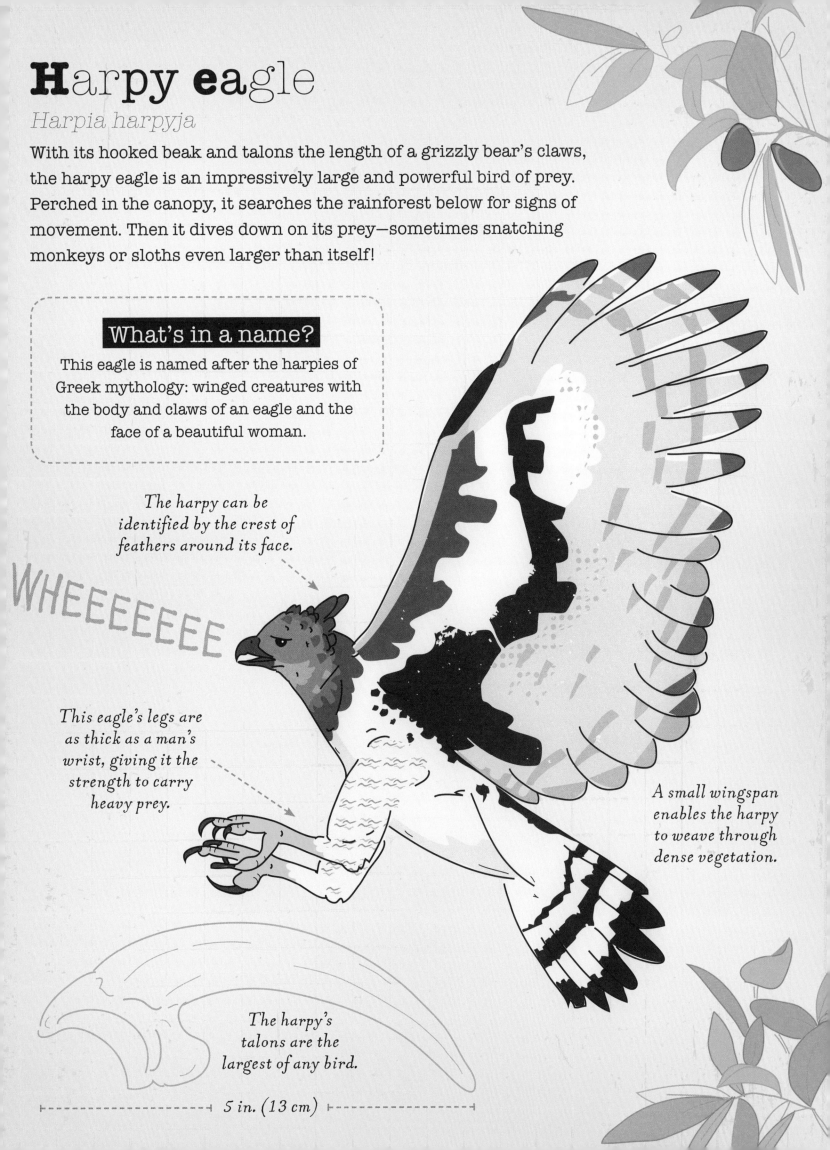

Magnificent frigate bird
Fregata magnificens

This tropical seabird has a glistening back of jet-black plumage, but in summer it also develops a peculiar balloonlike throat sack. An agile flyer, it lives a life of piracy, regularly stealing fish from other birds rather than hunting for itself!

A frigate bird attacking a smaller bird

Frigate birds can spend all their days soaring at heights of up to 1.5 miles (2,500 m).

Long, hooked bill

Clack Clack

Their feathers are barely waterproof, so the birds cannot sit on the sea for more than a minute.

Frigate birds are silent outside of their colonies.

The inflatable gular sac is only found in males. Its color fades outside the breeding season.

Chick

Females lay one egg every couple of years. It can take up to a year to raise a single youngster.

Blue-footed booby

Sula nebouxii

This clumsy bird uses its sky-blue feet for the all-important job of attracting a mate. Comically marching and lifting its legs, it performs lengthy courtship dances every year. The bluer a booby's feet, the more attractive it will be! Boobies also use their big, clownlike feet to keep their eggs warm until they hatch.

Boobies feed on schooling fish such as anchovies, sardines, and mackerel.

Folding their wings behind them, boobies can dive at nearly 60 mph (100 km/h) and plummet up to 80 ft (25 m) under the water after fish.

Pairs mate for life.

Boobies lift their feet and spread their wings as part of their courtship dance.

Vibrant blue coloring is a good indicator of a bird's physical condition.

What's in a name?

The name booby comes from the Spanish word *bobo*, meaning "clumsy" or "clown." This refers to the bird's awkward motion on land.

Hummingbirds

Trochilidae

These jewel-bright birds are some of the smallest in the animal kingdom. In flight, they are a blur of glittering feathers, their wings beating faster than the eye can see. This motion gives hummingbirds the unique ability to hover in midair, meaning they can get to the choicest flowers and linger there as they feed. Their long beaks can then reach deep inside the flowers to sip their nectar.

Iridescent pink flashes on the throat and head

Bee hummingbird eggs are just the size of a pea.

2 in. (5 cm)

Bee hummingbird

Mellisuga helenae

The minuscule bee hummingbird is the smallest bird in the world. It is just 2 inches (5 cm) long and weighs less than a penny.

The bee hummingbird beats its wings 80 times per second, rising to 200 when it wants to impress a mate.

It also has the fastest heart rate in the world at 1,260 beats per minute.

Sword-billed hummingbird

Ensifera ensifera

This top-heavy species is the only bird with a bill longer than its body. This means it can reach right into the deepest flowers—but it can make balancing hard work!

Long tongue

3 in. (8 cm)

Hummingbird bill shapes and sizes vary depending on the flower the species drinks from most.

The sword-billed's beak is so long that it has to preen its feathers with its feet.

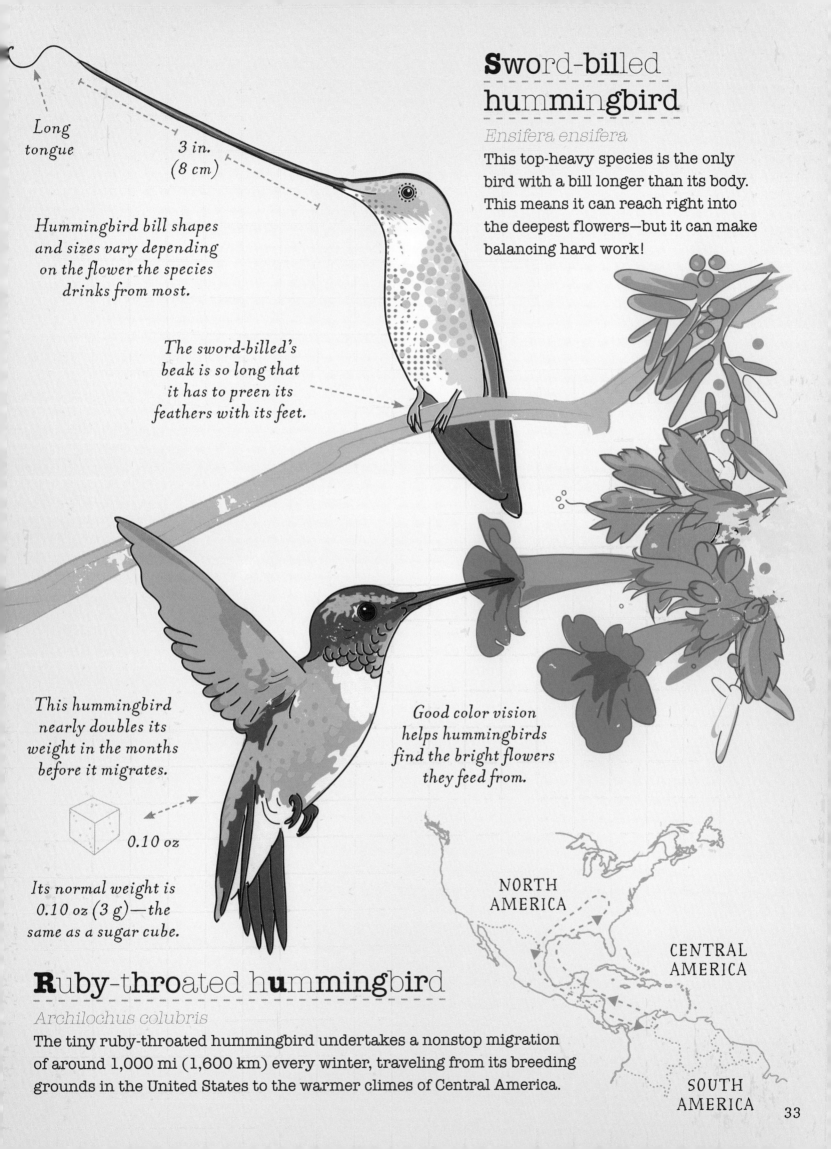

This hummingbird nearly doubles its weight in the months before it migrates.

0.10 oz

Its normal weight is 0.10 oz (3 g)—the same as a sugar cube.

Good color vision helps hummingbirds find the bright flowers they feed from.

NORTH AMERICA

CENTRAL AMERICA

SOUTH AMERICA

Ruby-throated hummingbird

Archilochus colubris

The tiny ruby-throated hummingbird undertakes a nonstop migration of around 1,000 mi (1,600 km) every winter, traveling from its breeding grounds in the United States to the warmer climes of Central America.

33

Toco toucan

Ramphastos toco

Living high among the branches of tropical forests, toucans are best known for their long, often colorful bills, which enable them to pluck fruits and berries from hard-to-reach places. The toco toucan has the largest bill to body size of any bird. Its bill is nearly a third of the toucan's total length.

The bill is light, as gaps in the bone are filled with a spongy tissue called keratin.

Toucans only have small wings. They can fly short distances but tend to hop about instead.

25 in. (63 cm)

Long beaks enable birds to reach into tree holes or pick hanging fruit.

Toco toucans have a dark body, white bib, and long, orange bill.

Keeping cool

Arteries in the bill allow toucans to quickly cool down, distributing and releasing heat, just like elephants release heat through their large ears.

Toucans mostly eat berries and fruits, but they also eat insects, frogs, and even birds' eggs.

Tree frog

Macaws

Psittacidae

Macaws are the largest members of the parrot family, easily spotted thanks to their majestic tails and dazzling rainbow colors. These clever birds are thought to have the same intelligence as a four-year-old child: They can recognize shapes and colors, and they can even mimic human speech.

The featherless skin around the eyes has patterning as unique as a fingerprint.

The long, scaly tongue contains a single bone.

Scarlet macaw

Ara macao

Like many other parrots, scarlet macaws mate for life. More unusually, they also eat clay, which helps them digest other parts of their diet.

Curved beak

Strong toes

Endangered

Deforestation and the illegal pet trade mean that several species of macaw are now listed as endangered.

Hyacinth macaw

Anodorhynchus hyacinthinus

The largest parrot on the planet, the hyacinth macaw has a wingspan of over 3 feet (1 m). Its curved beak is used to open nuts and fruits. It is so strong it can crack open a coconut!

Coconut

Hoatzin

Opisthocomus hoazin

The hoatzin spends most of its day grazing on leaves and fruit high above the swamps of the Amazon. In order to survive on its meager diet, it has an abnormally large digestive system, fermenting food in order to extract all the nutrients from it. The smell this makes has led to the hoatzins' unfortunate nickname: "stinkbirds"!

Spiky head crest

Hoatzins live in noisy social groups of up to 40 birds, which make a chorus of grunts and hissing noises.

Because of their heavy digestive system, hoatzins can only glide short distances.

Enlarged "crop" where food is fermented

Hisss

Crocodiles lurk beneath nests, hoping to catch a chick.

Chicks have tiny claws on their wings so they can climb to safety if they slip from the nest. The claws are lost once the chicks learn to fly.

Question of digestion

Fermentation of food takes place in a crop, or pouch, below the throat. It can take 45 hours for food to pass through the digestive system.

Resplendent quetzal

Pharomachrus mocinno

With its iridescent green plumage, the resplendent quetzal shines like a jewel in the Central American rainforest. Long revered as sacred by the ancient Aztec and Maya peoples, males grow two long tail feathers, which they use as part of an elaborate courtship performance to impress a female.

The female has slightly different coloring and shorter tail coverts.

Female

Male

Wild avocado

Adults feed mostly on fruit, especially avocados, but they also eat insects and other small animals.

In mating season, males grow two long "covert" feathers.

Pairs carve a hollow inside rotting trees, where they rear their young.

A place of safety

Much of the quetzals' habitat is being destroyed, but their numbers are growing in protected areas. Farmers are even encouraged to grow wild avocados for them.

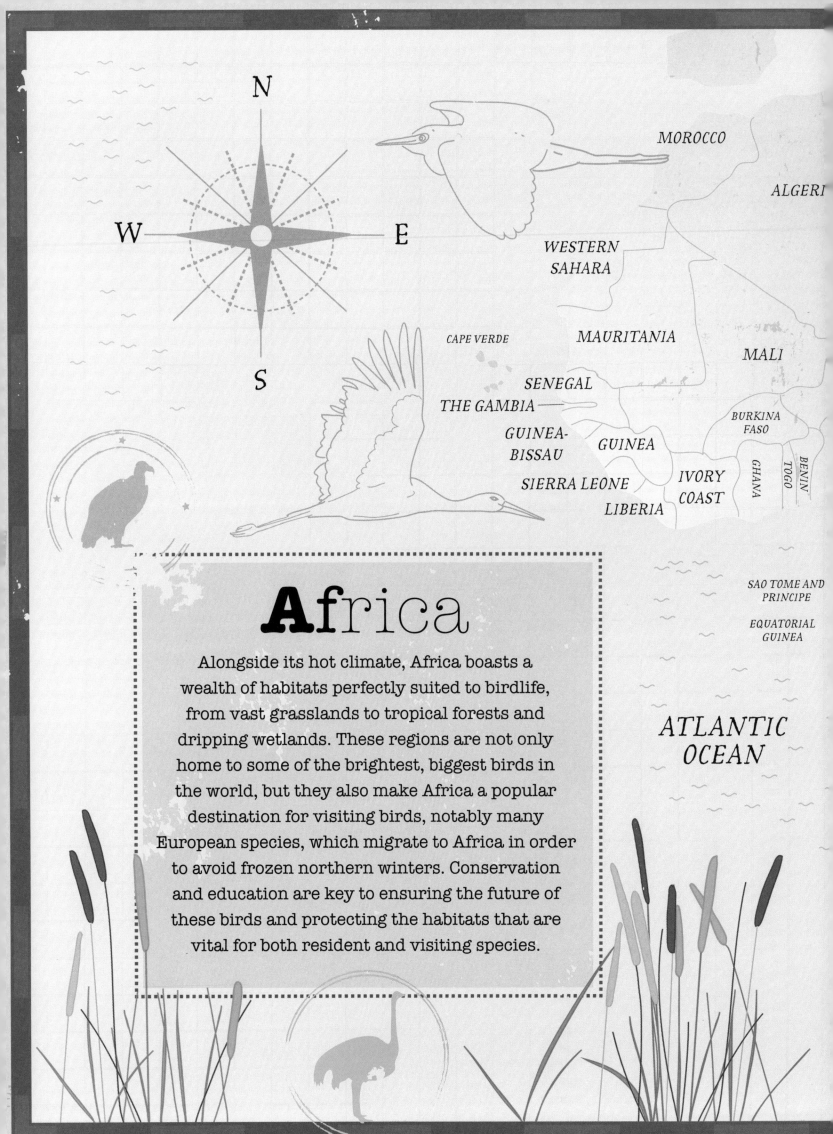

MOROCCO

ALGERI

WESTERN
SAHARA

CAPE VERDE

MAURITANIA

MALI

SENEGAL

THE GAMBIA —

BURKINA
FASO

GUINEA-
BISSAU

GUINEA

SIERRA LEONE

IVORY
COAST

GHANA

TOGO

BENIN

LIBERIA

SAO TOME AND
PRINCIPE

EQUATORIAL
GUINEA

ATLANTIC
OCEAN

Africa

Alongside its hot climate, Africa boasts a wealth of habitats perfectly suited to birdlife, from vast grasslands to tropical forests and dripping wetlands. These regions are not only home to some of the brightest, biggest birds in the world, but they also make Africa a popular destination for visiting birds, notably many European species, which migrate to Africa in order to avoid frozen northern winters. Conservation and education are key to ensuring the future of these birds and protecting the habitats that are vital for both resident and visiting species.

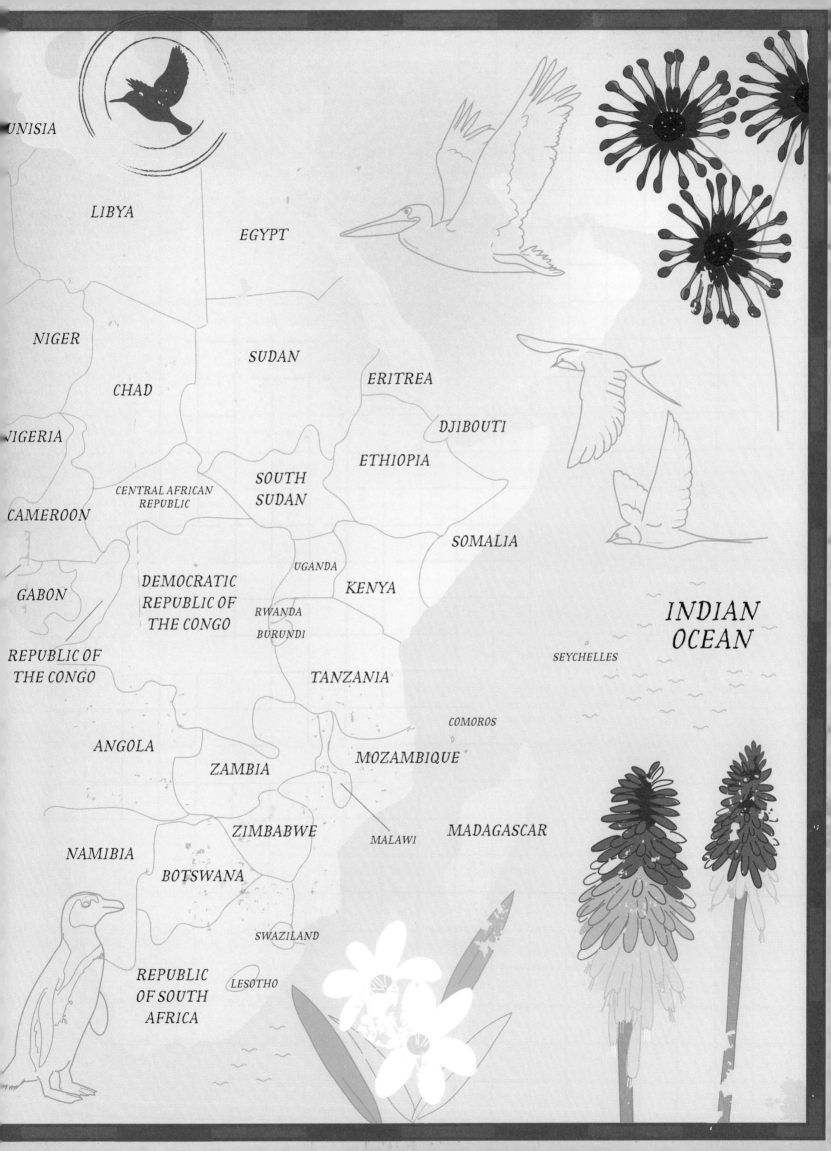

Ostrich
Struthio camelus

With its elegant neck, thick fan of feathers, and long, muscular legs, the mighty ostrich holds the title of the tallest and heaviest bird. It weighs roughly the same as a baby elephant and stands taller than a man. Due to its great weight, it is completely flightless, but it can run at impressive speeds of up to 43 miles (70 km) an hour.

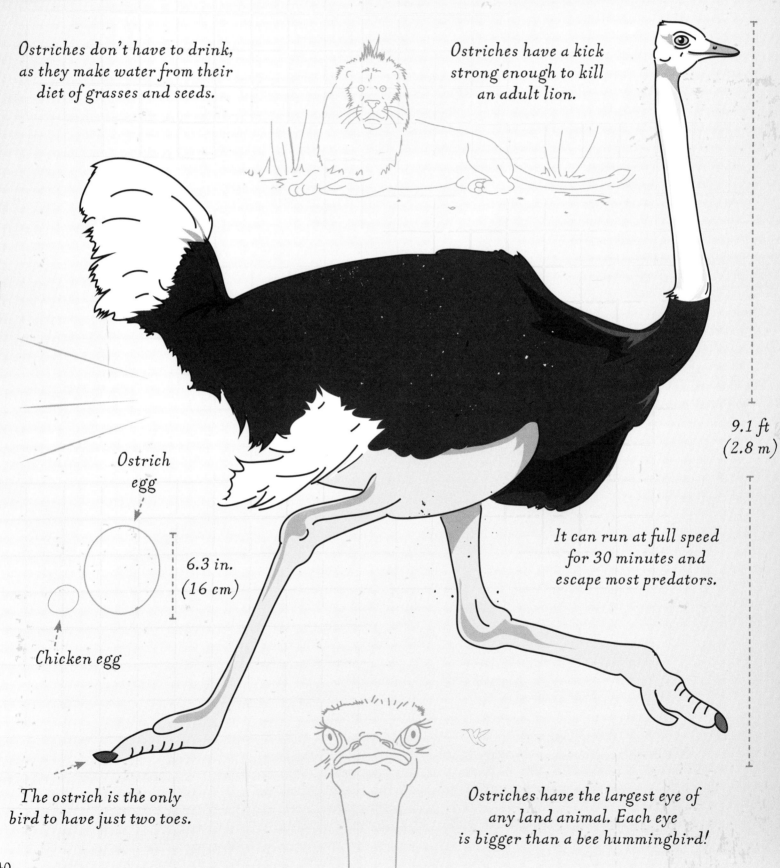

Ostriches don't have to drink, as they make water from their diet of grasses and seeds.

Ostriches have a kick strong enough to kill an adult lion.

Ostrich egg

6.3 in. (16 cm)

Chicken egg

9.1 ft (2.8 m)

It can run at full speed for 30 minutes and escape most predators.

The ostrich is the only bird to have just two toes.

Ostriches have the largest eye of any land animal. Each eye is bigger than a bee hummingbird!

African pygmy goose

Nettapus auritus

At 1 foot (30 cm) long, this pretty bird is the smallest waterfowl in the world. Despite its name, it is more closely related to ducks than geese. Like wood ducks, it likes to nest high in tree trunks, but it will sometimes nest in termite mounds or even thatched roofs!

The pygmy goose is also called a perching duck, as it tends to sit on branches over water.

The species has a short, high bill like that of a goose.

Males have a white face and green ear patches.

It lives across all of Africa except for the Sahara Desert.

Male

Females have grayer faces with dark eye patches.

Female

1 ft
(30 cm)

This goose lives in swamps, rivers, and lakes, feeding on water lily seeds and insects.

Spot**t**ed **sa**n**d**grouse

Pterocles senegallus

Perfectly camouflaged against its stony desert habitat, this pigeonlike
bird spends most of its time foraging on the ground. Here, it is vulnerable to
predators, so a "lookout bird" flies high above the flock and calls out at the first sign
of danger. At this warning, the other birds freeze, relying on their camouflage to
keep them completely concealed.

*Until the chicks can fly, the male
uses specially adapted breast
feathers to soak up water and
carry it back to his family.*

*The male can soak up to around
25 mL of water—about the
same as two tablespoons.*

Queet - queet - queet

*The male makes a
"queet-queet" call to
announce his return.*

Male

Female

*Dark markings on the
tail and wings provide
excellent camouflage.*

*Chicks hatch with soft down and
are already well camouflaged.*

Black-crowned crane
Balearica pavonina

This tall bird's dainty head is topped with a magnificent crown of yellow feathers. Pairs dance every year to strengthen their bond, bowing their necks and leaping high into the air. This is accompanied by deep booming calls, which are made with a balloonlike sack in the birds' throats.

Stiff golden feathers or "crown"

Honk Honk

Wonk Wonk

The gular sac expands to make a booming call.

Vulnerable

Black-crowned cranes are in decline due to the destruction of their wetland habitat. They are officially classed as "vulnerable."

Cranes stamp their feet as they walk to flush out more insects.

Birds usually dance in the morning. Once bonded, they stay together for life.

Energetic union dance

3 ft
(1 m)

A long hind toe helps grasp onto branches when perching.

Grasshopper

Shoebill

Balaeniceps rex

This tall, sly-looking bird uses its large bill as a formidable weapon, crushing and even decapitating prey in one swift move. Stalking the warm, swampy waters of eastern Africa, the shoebill can stay motionless for minutes on end as it lies in wait, ready to ambush.

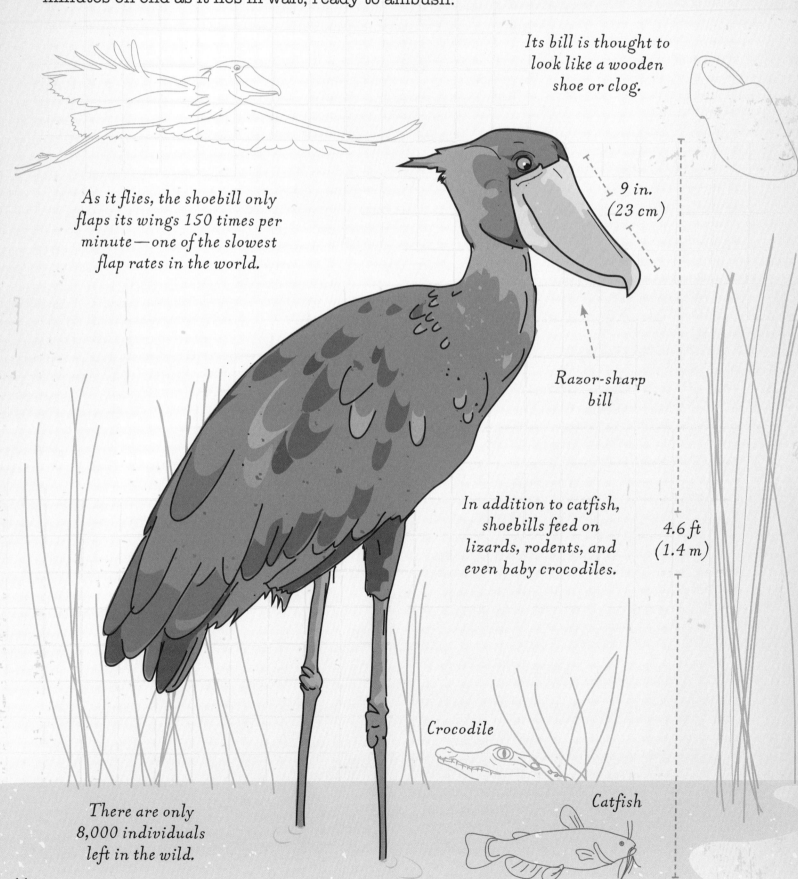

Its bill is thought to look like a wooden shoe or clog.

As it flies, the shoebill only flaps its wings 150 times per minute—one of the slowest flap rates in the world.

9 in. (23 cm)

Razor-sharp bill

In addition to catfish, shoebills feed on lizards, rodents, and even baby crocodiles.

4.6 ft (1.4 m)

Crocodile

There are only 8,000 individuals left in the wild.

Catfish

Lappet-faced vulture

Torgos tracheliotos

The enormous lappet-faced vulture is the largest vulture in Africa, with a wingspan of about 9.5 feet (2.9 m). Scavenging on dead and decaying bodies, it uses its strong, hooked beak to crush bones and tear through body parts such as bones and tendons, which would be inedible to most animals.

Its powerful beak can tear tendons and thick animal skin.

Keen eyes can spot carcasses up to 0.6 mi (1 km) away.

9.5 ft
(2.9 m)

The bald head and neck are easy to clean. Vultures often visit waterholes to wash after eating.

Fleshy folds of skin called lappets

The crop below the throat can hold up to 3.3 lb (1.5 kg) of meat— about the same as a whole chicken!

Endangered

Vultures worldwide face habitat destruction, pollution, hunting, and poisoning. The lappet-faced vulture is currently listed as endangered.

This vulture will even fight off a jackal to secure a meal.

Secretary bird
Sagittarius serpentarius

This towering bird is the only ground-dwelling bird of prey in the world. Walking up to 18.5 mi (30 km) a day, it silently searches for insects, mammals, and venomous snakes hiding in the grass. To make a kill, it stamps on its victim with great force, crushing it then swallowing it whole.

What's in a name?

The secretary bird is probably named after its resemblance to eighteenth-century secretaries, who would tuck goose-quill pens behind their ears. This image may have sprung to mind when Europeans first saw the birds.

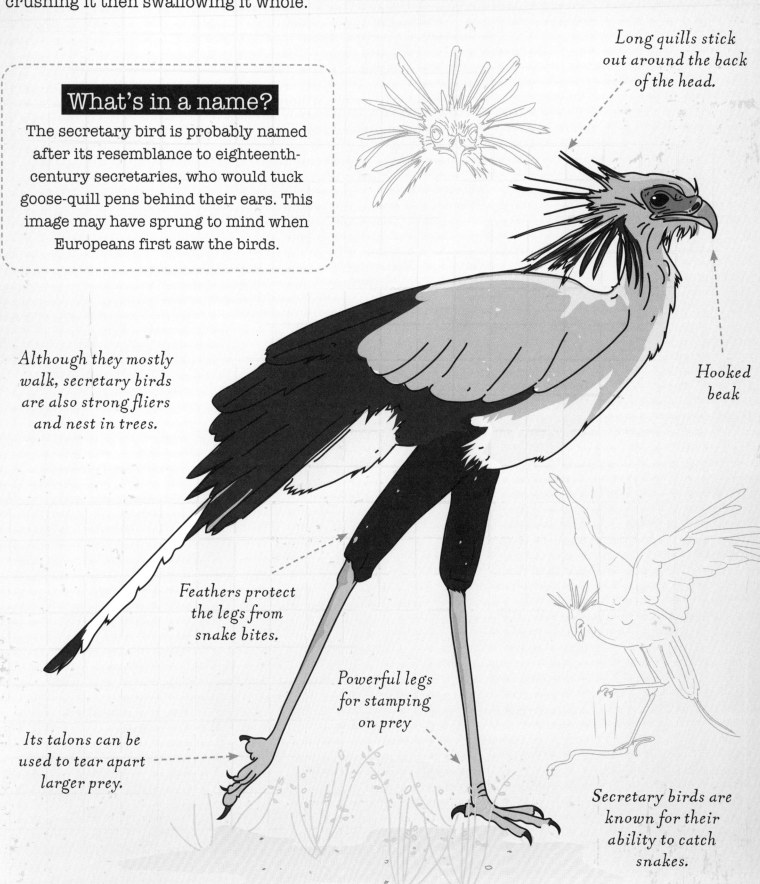

Long quills stick out around the back of the head.

Hooked beak

Although they mostly walk, secretary birds are also strong fliers and nest in trees.

Feathers protect the legs from snake bites.

Its talons can be used to tear apart larger prey.

Powerful legs for stamping on prey

Secretary birds are known for their ability to catch snakes.

Schalow's turaco
Tauraco schalowi

An elegant copper-green bird living high above the forest floor, the turaco has a clever way of getting about. Dense treetop vegetation makes forest flying difficult, but the turaco is a dexterous climber, easily clambering between branches as it forages for fruit. It even has a special "climbing toe" to give it better grip.

The Schalow's turaco can easily be identified thanks to its white head crest.

kaaar
Kaaar
kaaar

The patterning in the turaco's plumage comes from two copper pigments not thought to be found in any other variety of bird.

The small round wings are only used for short flights.

Turacos rarely, if ever, land on the ground.

A special joint enables the outer toe to swivel forward or backward, giving the bird a secure but flexible grip.

Northern carmine bee-eater

Merops nubicus

These nimble birds feed mostly on bees and other flying insects, which they catch in midair and beat against the ground to remove their stingers. Northern carmine bee-eaters are named after the pigment "carmine," which matches their bright red plumage.

A ring of fire

Bee-eaters often fly to the sites of wild fires, where they circle the edges of the flames, waiting to catch insects as they make their escape.

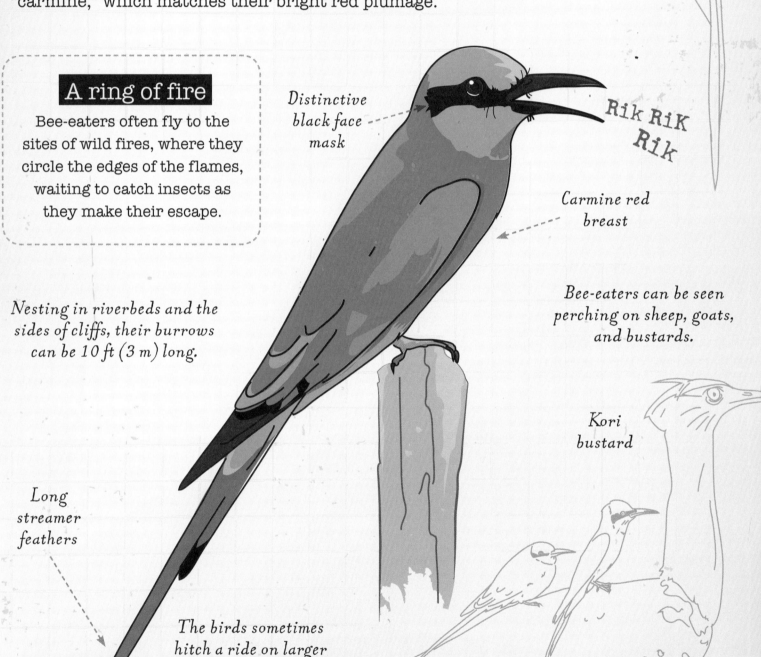

Distinctive black face mask

Rik Rik Rik

Carmine red breast

Bee-eaters can be seen perching on sheep, goats, and bustards.

Nesting in riverbeds and the sides of cliffs, their burrows can be 10 ft (3 m) long.

Kori bustard

Long streamer feathers

The birds sometimes hitch a ride on larger animals so they can eat the insects kicked up as they walk.

Barn swallow
Hirundo rustica

Barn swallows travel enormous distances every year, moving north to south with the changing seasons. On their annual migrations, they can fly up to 200 mi (320 km) a day—the equivalent of 7.5 marathon races. As they fly, they eat and drink without missing a wingbeat, swooping low to sip water or chasing insect prey through the air.

Before animal migration was understood, people used to think swallows disappeared because they buried themselves in mud!

Mud

Grass

They beat their wings eight times a second.

Cuplike nests are made from mud and lined with grass. They can take 1,200 trips to complete.

Long, forked tail

EUROPE

AFRICA

Red throat

A long journey
The barn swallows seen in Africa migrate all the way from Europe every year, a round-trip journey of about 7,200 mi (11,600 km).

The barn swallow is the most widespread species of swallow in the world.

Barn swallows also migrate in other parts of the world.

Southern **mas**ked **wea**ver

Ploceus velatus

This yellow songbird is a master builder. Every spring, males get to work weaving blades of grass into delicately domed nests, which hang high in the trees over rivers and ponds. But females aren't easy to impress, and only the very best nests will do. Males sometimes build up to 25 nests to attract a mate.

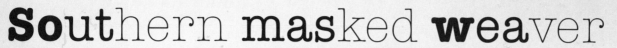

Termites

Its black face mask gives this bird its name.

Nests can take from a few hours to a few days to construct.

Weaver birds mostly eat grass seeds but sometimes eat insects such as termites.

Grasses and leaves are woven and knotted together.

Its tail gives the bird balance while it is weaving.

Weaver birds sometimes strip all the branches for 6-10 feet (2-3 m) around their nest.

The nest's entrance is made at the very last stage, after the female has selected a nest.

Female inspecting nests

Entrance

Cape sugarbird
Promerops cafer

The cape sugarbird has a taste for all things sweet and feeds almost entirely on the sugary nectar of protea flowers, visiting up to 300 of them a day. As soon as the flowers bloom, the sugarbird starts to nest. This gives the adults plenty of food, but the flowers also attract insects that the parents can feed to their chicks.

Frrt-Frrt

Beak is curved for reaching into flowers.

Floral harmony

As sugarbirds feed, their feathers are dusted with pollen, which they carry between plants. This pollinates flowers so that they can grow seeds and reproduce.

When the male flies, its wings make a fluttering noise, which attracts females.

Cape sugarbirds live in fynbos regions: a type of shrubland that only grows on the western tip of South Africa.

The male's tail is twice as long as its body.

Fynbos plants

ICELAND

ATLANTIC
OCEAN

SWEDEN

FINLAND

NORWAY

ESTONIA

LATVIA

IRELAND

DENMARK

LITHUANIA

UNITED
KINGDOM

BELARU

NETHERLANDS

POLAND

GERMANY

BELGIUM

LUXEMBOURG

CZECH
REPUBLIC

SLOVAKIA

LIECHTENSTEIN

AUSTRIA

HUNGARY

FRANCE

SWITZERLAND

SLOVENIA

ROMANIA

CROATIA

SAN MARINO

BOSNIA AND
HERZEGOVINA

SERBIA

PORTUGAL

SPAIN

ANDORRA

MONACO

Corsica
(FRANCE)

ITALY

BULGARIA

MONTENEGRO

KOSOVO

MACEDONIA

Sardinia
(ITALY)

ALBANIA

GREECE

Sicily
(ITALY)

MEDITERRANEAN
SEA

MALTA

Europe

Warm in the south, mild in the middle, and cold in the north, Europe is also one of the most developed continents in the world. Many of its birds have adapted to an urban environment, nesting under eaves or on top of skyscrapers and finding that urban temperatures are warmer all year round. However, others still migrate with the changing seasons. In certain regions, hunting and trapping still threaten wildlife, as do some farming practices. But with international birding groups delivering much-needed data, this decline in Europe's bird numbers can still be stopped.

RUSSIA

UKRAINE

MOLDOVA

GEORGIA

TURKEY

CYPRUS

N

W   E

S

Bewick's swan

Cygnus columbianus bewickii

The elegant Bewick's swan spends each summer breeding in the
Arctic tundra of northern Russia. But to avoid the region's freezing winters,
huge flocks fly south each autumn—some to northern Europe, and others to
China and Japan. At around 4,350 miles (7,000 km) each way—nearly the
length of the Great Wall of China—it is the longest migration of any swan.

*This social swan forms strong
family bonds, with pairs staying
together for many years.*

*When migrating, the first bird
to arrive waits patiently for its
partner to join it.*

*The yellow and black beak patterns
are unique to each swan and can be
used to identify individuals—just
like human fingerprints.*

Yellow bill
patch

*Although small
for a swan, these
birds have a loud,
musical honk.*

Short square
tail

honk

*Chicks, called cygnets, are gray
when they hatch, then turn
snowy white as they mature.*

Great crested grebe

Podiceps cristatus

Once favored for its feathers, which were used to decorate hats, the great crested grebe has survived heavy hunting and can now be admired in the wild. With its slender neck and ornate ear tufts, it is always a spectacle, especially when performing its extravagant courtship displays.

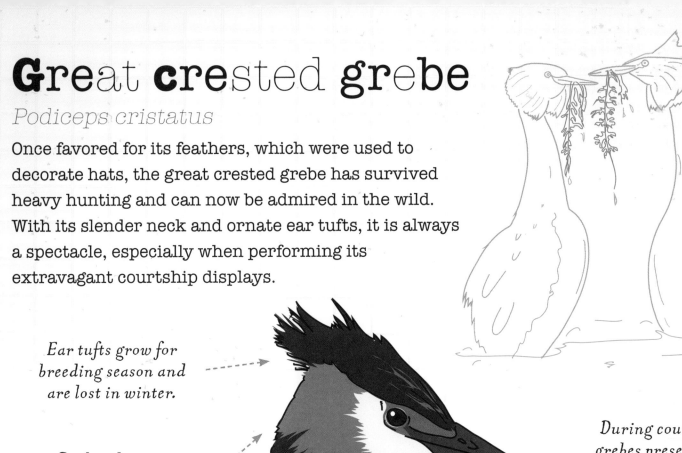

Ear tufts grow for breeding season and are lost in winter.

Dark red eyes improve underwater vision.

Grebes are strong divers, staying underwater for up to a minute.

During courtship, grebes present each other with bouquets of plants, which can be used for building a nest.

Long, spearlike bill

Grebes are unable to walk well on land and require a running start to take to the air.

Striped chicks often hitch a ride on their parents' backs.

Fashionable feathers

The great crested grebe was nearly wiped out in Britain in the nineteenth century when ladies started wearing grebe feathers. Pressure from a group of women (later to become the Royal Society for the Protection of Birds) changed attitudes and saved the birds.

Grey heron
Ardea cinerea

This long-legged wading bird can often be seen motionless at the edges of ponds and rivers, patiently waiting to spot movement in the water. The moment any small animal passes, the heron moves with lightning speed, snatching up prey as large as small ducks.

As herons fly, their legs stretch out and their long necks curve back.

Its long, sharp bill can skewer larger prey like a spear.

Herons nest in colonies known as "heronries," high in tall trees. They return to the same spot each year.

Krornk

By quickly straightening its neck, a heron can lash out with great speed.

Reed warbler

Long legs enable the heron to move easily in the water or on land.

Tench

Herons feed on fish, amphibians, mammals, and birds. Small prey is swallowed whole, while larger prey is taken to the shore to eat.

Frog

Common cuckoo
Cuculus canorus

The jaunty call of the cuckoo is a sure sign that spring has started, as the birds arrive in Europe from their wintering grounds farther south. The cuckoo lays its egg in the nest of an unsuspecting bird, which will incubate the cuckoo egg along with its own eggs. But once the cuckoo hatches, it will kill the rest of them to ensure its own survival.

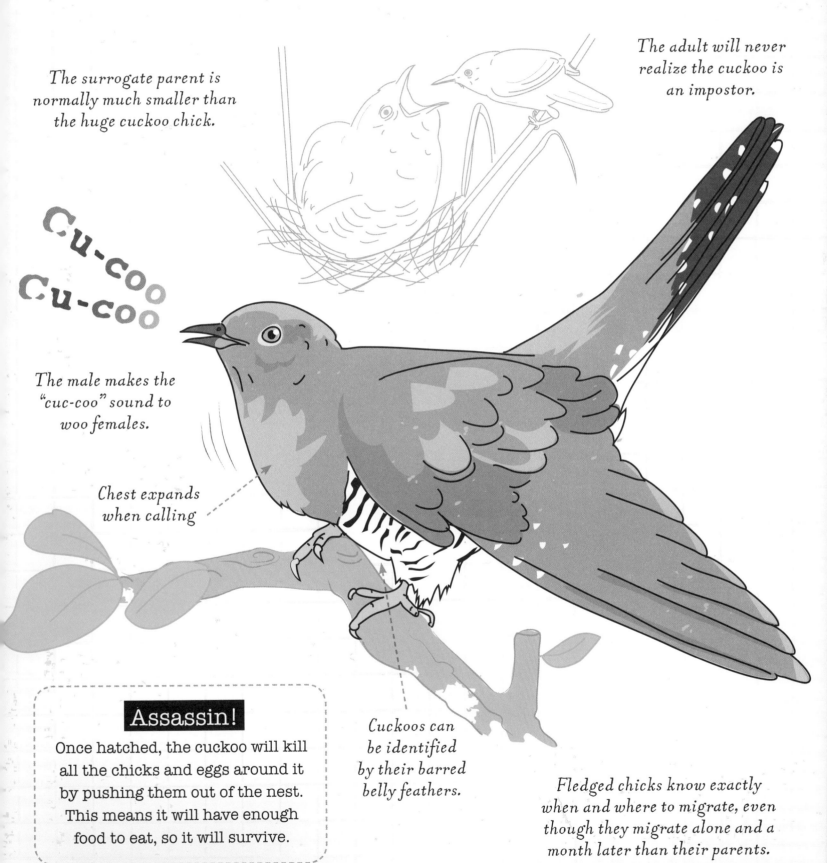

The surrogate parent is normally much smaller than the huge cuckoo chick.

The adult will never realize the cuckoo is an impostor.

Cu-coo
Cu-coo

The male makes the "cuc-coo" sound to woo females.

Chest expands when calling

Assassin!

Once hatched, the cuckoo will kill all the chicks and eggs around it by pushing them out of the nest. This means it will have enough food to eat, so it will survive.

Cuckoos can be identified by their barred belly feathers.

Fledged chicks know exactly when and where to migrate, even though they migrate alone and a month later than their parents.

Owls

Strigiformes

These nocturnal birds use their sharp senses and near-silent flight to hunt at night. Their round facial discs direct noises towards their ears, enabling them to pinpoint the exact location of prey, even in the dark. Their large eyes also give them excellent night-vision, and they can swivel their heads 270 degrees to look all around them.

The great gray owl has the largest facial disc of any bird of prey.

Front-facing eyes give good depth perception.

Owls cough up "pellets" containing the parts of their diet they cannot digest, such as bones and fur.

Pellet

Rodent skull

Most owls sleep during the day in crevices or even perched on branches.

Gray owls find their prey by listening for their heartbeats.

Great gray owl

Strix nebulosa

Found in Russia, Scandinavia, and North America, this owl is the largest by length in the world. It can hear small animals moving beneath snow up to 20 inches (50 cm) deep and can dive through the snow bank to catch them.

Vole

The right ear takes in sounds from above.

The left ear takes in sounds from below.

Skkkreechhh

Barn owls screech instead of hooting like other owls.

Large wings and soft feathers enable nearly silent flight.

Barn owl

Tyto alba

The barn owl is the most widespread owl in the world, found on every continent apart from Antarctica. It can easily be identified by its beautiful heart-shaped facial disc and rusty golden plumage.

A barn owl can eat up to four rodents a night.

Shrew

Field mouse

Lemon-yellow eyes

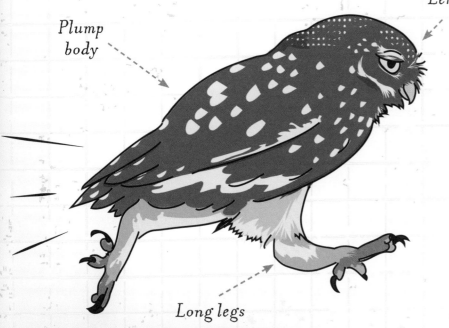

Plump body

Little owl

Athene noctua

Little owls live in southern Europe, where the weather is warmer. They are quick runners and prefer to hunt on foot, often chasing their prey through the undergrowth during daylight hours.

Long legs

Atlantic puffin
Fratercula arctica

Nicknamed the "clowns of the sea," these small seabirds are known for their bright, parrotlike beaks. Puffins spend most of their lives in the open ocean, but every summer they gather in the thousands on coastlines and offshore islands. Here they pair off and build their nests underground. Some couples may be together for 20 years!

Puffins are excellent swimmers, diving over 200 feet (60 m) deep. Their beaks can hold up to 12 fish at a time.

Sardines

Beaks are gray in winter but change color in spring to attract a mate.

Webbed feet for swimming underwater

aRR

A baby puffin is called a "puffling."

Puffins only lay one egg each year.

60

Great cormorant

Phalacrocorax carbo

This black, almost reptilian-looking waterbird can often be seen perching on posts and buoys, with its wings outstretched and drying in the sun. These talented fishers can dive deep underwater in pursuit of prey, and a single bird can consume its entire body weight in fish in just one day.

Slender, hooked beak

This pose is thought to help cormorants dry their wings after diving, though some scientists think it helps the birds digest their food.

Adults' coats have a blue or green sheen to their black plumage.

Webbed feet for swimming underwater

Stiff tail

Acid droppings

Cormorants build their nests on cliffs or high in trees near coastlines. But the birds' droppings are so highly acidic that they will kill their nest tree in just a few years!

Cormorants live around coastlines, lakes, rivers, and estuaries.

Eurasian hoopoe
Upupa epops

Named after the "oop-oop" call it makes, the hoopoe can often be seen sunbathing in warmer parts of Europe, as well as in Africa and as far east as Asia. It has an exotic appearance, with its huge head crest and zebra-striped wings, and it can produce a surprisingly powerful stench to ward off predators.

Hoopoes stretch their heads back to sunbathe.

Crest rising

Hoopoes only half-close their wings after beating them, so they have a wave-like flight like a butterfly.

This sun-loving bird can also be seen taking dust baths.

These birds are mostly silent outside the breeding season.

The crest rises up when the bird lands.

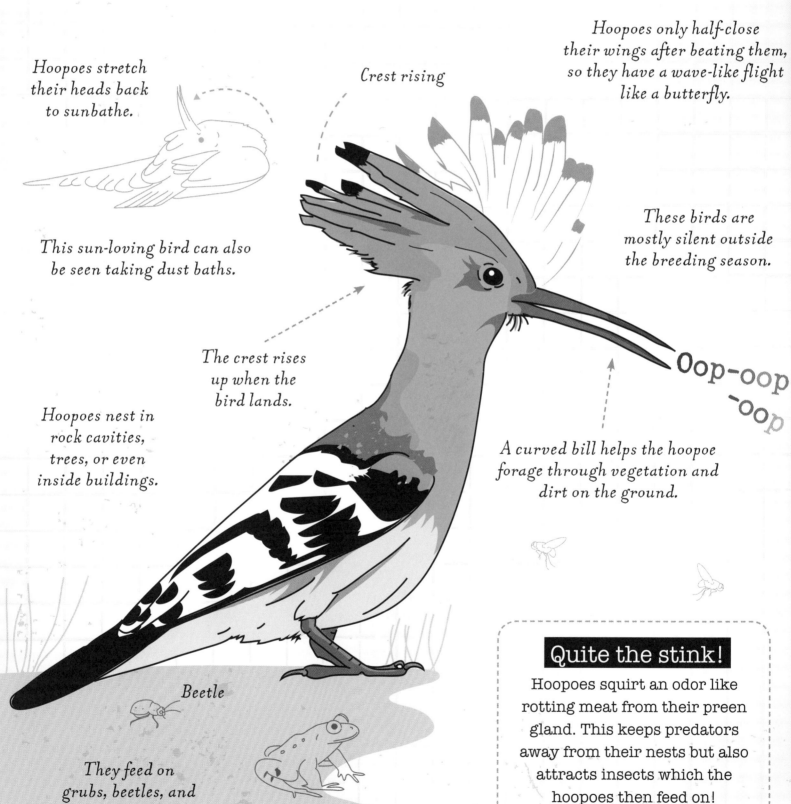

Hoopoes nest in rock cavities, trees, or even inside buildings.

A curved bill helps the hoopoe forage through vegetation and dirt on the ground.

Oop-oop-oop

Beetle

They feed on grubs, beetles, and sometimes frogs.

Frog

Quite the stink!

Hoopoes squirt an odor like rotting meat from their preen gland. This keeps predators away from their nests but also attracts insects which the hoopoes then feed on!

Common kingfisher

Alcedo atthis

Most people will only ever see a kingfisher as a flash of turquoise, whizzing past them near rivers and lakes. This is because kingfishers move with incredible speed, diving at over 55 mph (90 km/h) as they plummet into the water to catch a fish. Each bird has its own small territory where it hunts, using its dagger-shaped bill to spear larger prey.

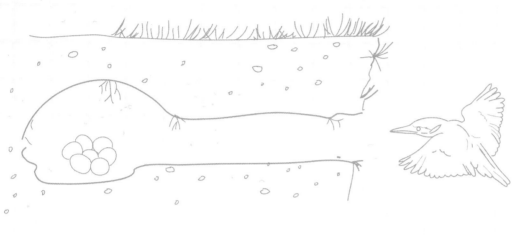

Kingfishers burrow into riverbanks or under trees, making tunnels toward their nest chambers.

Nests get dirty quickly; the adults even have to wash in water to remove the filth!

A third transparent eyelid protects the kingfisher's eyes when it is underwater.

Kingfishers hit their prey against a branch to stun it, then swallow it whole.

During courtship, the male presents the female with a gift of fish.

Common starling
Sturnus vulgaris

Glossy black starlings live across much of the world and in many urban areas. When the weather grows cool, they gather in extraordinary numbers, sweeping through the sky like a cloud of smoke. The largest flock ever recorded is thought to have included over six million birds—that's more than the population of Denmark!

Murmuration

Sometimes flocks form spectacular flight patterns called "murmurations." The most impressive are thought to happen when danger is near. The birds' tight formation and fast, coordinated movements make it hard for a predator to single out one target.

Starlings raised in captivity can mimic human speech!

Chet Chet

Starlings roost together in groups of up to a million!

The bill is black in winter and yellow in summer.

Newly molted birds have white spots all over their black plumage. These fade in winter.

On closer inspection, starlings' black feathers have a sheen of iridescent green and purple.

Short tail

Tits
Paridae and Aegithalidae

Tits are a big family of perching birds with small, plump bodies. Found widely across the Northern Hemisphere and Africa, they are known for their intelligence and are only outsmarted by crows and parrots. They learn from each other and are even thought to use herbs such as lavender to disinfect their nests!

Tits are light and acrobatic.

Blue tit

Cyanistes caeruleus

This small, brightly colored tit is a favorite garden visitor. During winter, it lives in family groups to help it search for food.

The male is brighter than the female.

zee zee zee

Long-tailed tit

Aegithalos caudatus

Fluffy and chatty, long-tailed tits live in small flocks, huddling for warmth as they roost together on long branches. Their nests are made from cobwebs, moss, and hair.

Crested tit

Lophophanes cristatus

Easily identified by its jaunty head crest and black-and-white face, the crested tit stores up food in autumn and goes back for it in winter months.

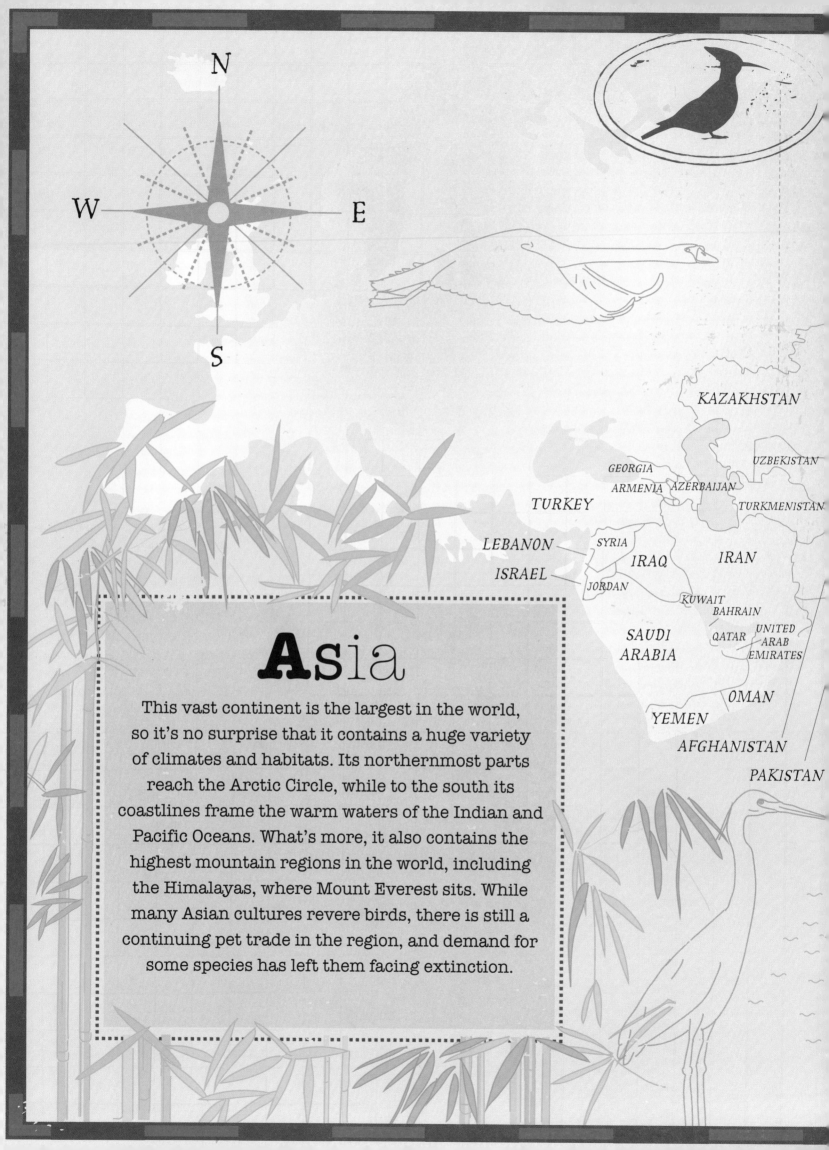

N

W E

S

KAZAKHSTAN

UZBEKISTAN

GEORGIA

ARMENIA   AZERBAIJAN

TURKMENISTAN

TURKEY

LEBANON   SYRIA

ISRAEL   IRAQ   IRAN

JORDAN

KUWAIT

BAHRAIN

SAUDI   QATAR   UNITED
ARABIA   ARAB
                      EMIRATES

YEMEN   OMAN

AFGHANISTAN

PAKISTAN

Asia

This vast continent is the largest in the world, so it's no surprise that it contains a huge variety of climates and habitats. Its northernmost parts reach the Arctic Circle, while to the south its coastlines frame the warm waters of the Indian and Pacific Oceans. What's more, it also contains the highest mountain regions in the world, including the Himalayas, where Mount Everest sits. While many Asian cultures revere birds, there is still a continuing pet trade in the region, and demand for some species has left them facing extinction.

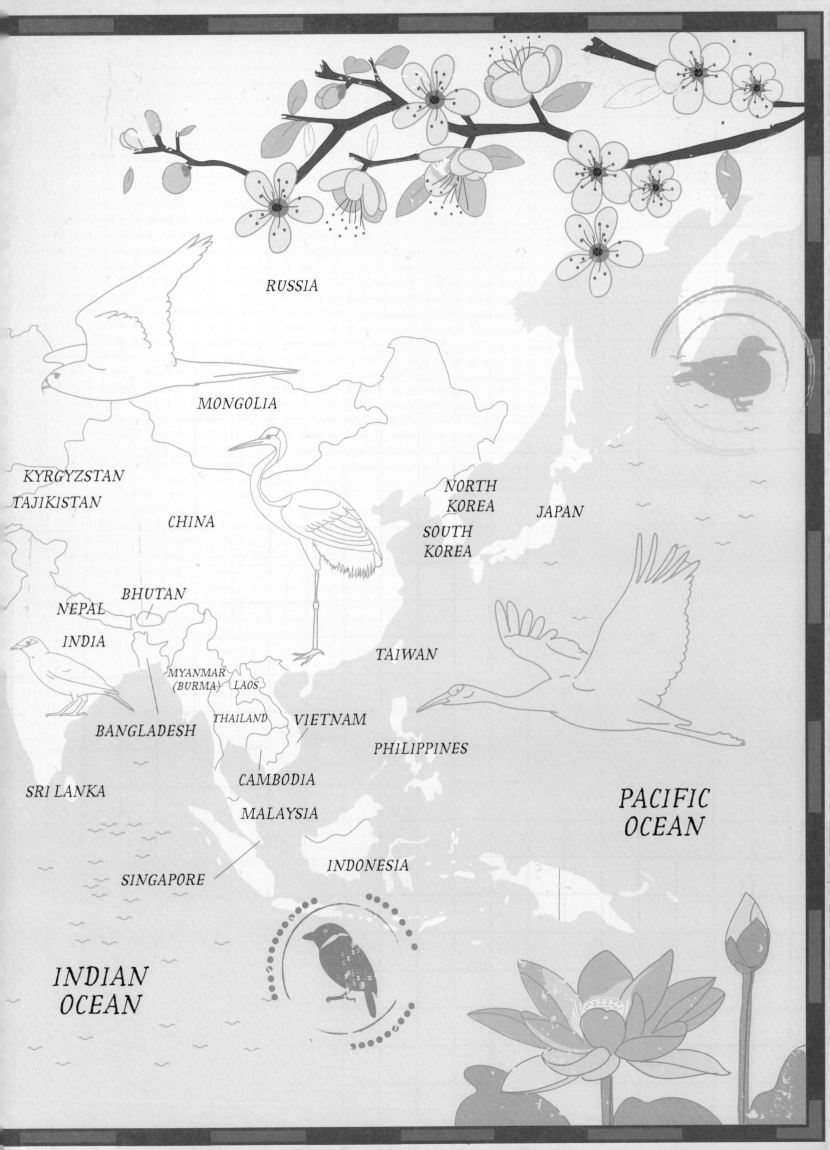

RUSSIA

MONGOLIA

KYRGYZSTAN

TAJIKISTAN

CHINA

NORTH
KOREA

SOUTH
KOREA

JAPAN

BHUTAN

NEPAL

INDIA

MYANMAR
(BURMA)

LAOS

TAIWAN

THAILAND

VIETNAM

BANGLADESH

PHILIPPINES

SRI LANKA

CAMBODIA

MALAYSIA

PACIFIC
OCEAN

INDONESIA

SINGAPORE

INDIAN
OCEAN

Mandarin duck
Aix galericulata

Described by some as the most beautiful duck in the world, the ornate mandarin has long been considered a symbol of faithfulness. In some parts of Korea, the birds are even given to couples on their wedding day! Despite their romantic image, they are like most ducks and only stay together for a single season.

Foul taste!

Mandarins are one of the only ducks not hunted for food anywhere in the world. This is because their meat is said to taste disgusting!

Male

The "sail" feathers are elongated flight feathers.

Ducklings leap from their tree nests onto the soft forest floor.

The female's colors keep her camouflaged.

Duckling

Female

After breeding season, males lose their colorful feathers. Other than their distinctive red beaks, they look just like the female.

Unlike most ducks, the mandarin has sharp claws for scrambling up trees to its nest.

Red junglefowl
Gallus gallus

This feisty wild bird is the ancestor of all domesticated chickens. Wandering free among the forests of Southeast Asia, flocks of junglefowl follow a strict "pecking order" with dominant males and females ruling the roost. Dominance is thought to be passed down from generation to generation, meaning pack leaders are often all from the same chicken family.

Junglefowl spend most of the day searching for food on the ground, but they fly up to roost in trees at night.

Comb

Cock-a-doodle-doo

Chickens were first domesticated around 10,000 years ago, and every domestic chicken in the world descends from the junglefowl. There are currently around 19 billion domestic chickens on the planet—that's nearly three to every human!

Hackles are long glossy feathers used to attract females.

Wattle

Female

Male

After molting in summer, males grow dull black feathers on their neck, known as "eclipse plumage."

This sharp spur is used for fighting other males.

Chick

Indian peafowl

Pavo cristatus

With their jewellike plumage and echoing calls, these birds are always the center of attention. Males, known as peacocks, have a flowing train of around 200 green feathers, each adorned with a shimmering eyespot in red, gold, and blue. When a female approaches, he spreads his train into a fan—males with the best trains are sure to attract the most mates.

Colorful eyespots on tail

Males also have a crown of feathers on the top of their head.

Tail feathers can grow up to 5 feet (1.5 m) long.

Peafowl only fly at night when they roost high up in trees.

PEE-OW · PEE-OW

Female

Male

Females are called peahens.

A group of two to five peahens, known as a harem, will all mate with the same peacock.

Greater flamingo

Phoenicopterus roseus

Wading through the warm shallows of coastal lagoons, flamingos spend
most of their days with their heads upside down in the water. Here they sift for food
as their long legs disturb tiny creatures hiding in the mud. Their diet of crustaceans
and algae from the lagoon gives the birds their distinctive coloring. Newborn birds
are white or gray and take up to three years to reach their adult color.

*The greater flamingo
is the largest and palest
of all flamingos.*

*Flamingos push
water out of their beaks,
trapping food in its
comblike edge.*

What's in a name?

The name flamingo comes
from the Spanish word
flamenco, meaning "fire."
This refers to the birds'
bright colors.

*Colonies of up to 20,000 flamingos
gather to breed. They perform
"marching parades," moving in
harmony to attract a partner.*

*Flamingos often balance on one
leg to maintain their temperature
when standing in cool water.*

Shrimp

Great white pelican
Pelecanus onocrotalus

This massive waterbird is best known for its yellow throat pouch—an expandable sack of skin that can hold up to three times the volume of its stomach. Working in groups, great white pelicans herd fish into the shallows where they are easily scooped from the water. In one deft movement, the bird then lifts its head, drains out the water, and tips the fish down its throat.

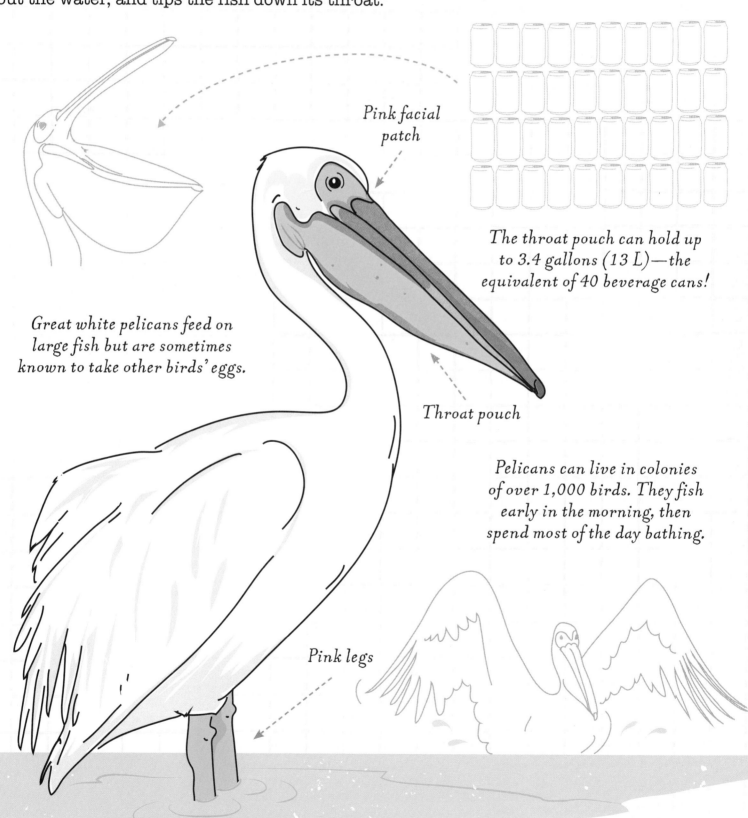

Pink facial patch

The throat pouch can hold up to 3.4 gallons (13 L)—the equivalent of 40 beverage cans!

Great white pelicans feed on large fish but are sometimes known to take other birds' eggs.

Throat pouch

Pelicans can live in colonies of over 1,000 birds. They fish early in the morning, then spend most of the day bathing.

Pink legs

Steller's sea eagle
Haliaeetus pelagicus

The rare sea eagle breeds only in northern Siberia before migrating south to Japan every autumn. There the winters are milder, and the eagles can still hunt their favorite prey, weaving between ice floes to snatch fish from the water's surface. The eagles that do not migrate will hunt inland, feeding on larger prey such as birds and small deer.

8.2 ft (2.5 m)

Eagles wait on waterside perches until they spy their prey.

3.3 ft (1 m)

Hooked bill with a high arch

The bottom of each foot is covered in bumpy "spiracles" to help grip slippery fish.

Sea eagles love to eat salmon.

Steller's sea eagles are also known to attack other birds in order to steal their catch.

National treasure

Steller's sea eagles are protected throughout their range, which is limited to Siberia and Japan. In Japan, they are even classified as an official National Treasure.

73

Peregrine falcon
Falco peregrinus

The fastest animal on the planet, the peregrine falcon is a formidable hunter, descending on prey at speeds faster than a racecar. It can survive in almost any habitat and lives on every continent except Antarctica. It is even known to live in urban landscapes, where towering buildings replace its usual cliff-top perches.

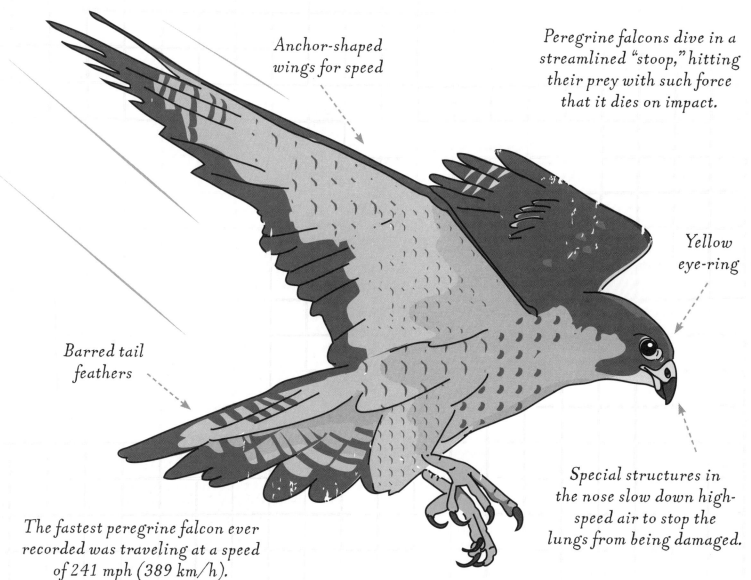

Anchor-shaped wings for speed

Peregrine falcons dive in a streamlined "stoop," hitting their prey with such force that it dies on impact.

Barred tail feathers

Yellow eye-ring

Special structures in the nose slow down high-speed air to stop the lungs from being damaged.

The fastest peregrine falcon ever recorded was traveling at a speed of 241 mph (389 km/h).

Pigeons only reach 55 mph (90 km/h), so they don't have a chance of out-flying a falcon.

What's in a name?

"Peregrine" is an old word for "wanderer," referring to the long migrations many falcons make. Some fly 15,500 miles (25,000 km) a year from the Arctic to South America and back—almost half the circumference of the world!

Rhinoceros hornbill
Buceros rhinoceros

These strange-looking birds have bright, hornlike "casques" on their beaks, which are used for feeding, amplifying calls, and building their unusual nests. Like many birds, they nest inside hollow trees, but as an extra precaution against predators, the male then seals his family inside the tree. He will pass food to them through an opening until the young are old enough to fly.

Males have red eyes, while females have white eyes.

The lightweight "casque" takes six years to reach its full size.

Like the rest of the bill, the casque is made from keratin—the same material as our fingernails.

The seal protects against predators such as snakes.

3 ft
(90 cm)

Bringing up baby

Once the female lays her eggs, the male seals the hollow with a mix of mud, fruit, and poop, leaving a tiny gap to pass food through. After six weeks, the female breaks out of the hollow, reseals it, and helps find food. The chicks will break out when they are old enough to take flight.

The hornbill's short legs are better suited to hopping than walking.

Wallcreeper
Tichodroma muraria

The agile wallcreeper inhabits mountainous regions across India, Nepal, and Tibet, where it scales near-vertical rock faces, searching for insects inside cracks and crevices. It breeds at altitudes of 3,200 to 9,800 feet (1,000-3,000 m), then descends to the lowlands in winter. This is when it is most often spotted, resting on the side of walls and buildings.

Its cup-shaped nest is made of grass and moss, tucked securely into crevices or caves.

Its long, slightly curved bill can reach into cracks in the rock to catch insects.

Most nests have a front and back entrance so birds can easily escape in case of danger.

The wallcreeper spreads its wings wide to help it balance as it climbs.

The male has a black throat and breast during breeding season.

Large feet and sharp, curved claws help the wallcreeper hang on to vertical rock faces.

Spider

Patterns on its wings resemble those of a butterfly.

Japanese white-eye
Zosterops japonicus

This energetic songbird flits effortlessly between its favorite cherry blossom flowers, sipping nectar and snatching insects from the air. A little acrobat, it is frequently seen hanging upside down from branches in order to reach its food. Outside of the breeding season, huge flocks are a common sight in gardens, parks, and woods, especially in Japan.

This little bird weighs 0.3 ounces (10 g)— about the same as a felt-tip pen.

Distinctive white eye ring

This species is called Mejiro in Japanese, which literally means "white eye."

There are 98 species of white-eye. Many small Asian islands have their own unique species!

Curved bill for reaching into flowers and grabbing insects

Blossom and bloom

Every spring, the festival of *Hanami* takes place across Japan, where people celebrate the cherry blossoms as they bloom. At the same time, flocks of white-eyes can also be seen enjoying the flowers' sweet nectar.

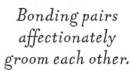

Bonding pairs affectionately groom each other.

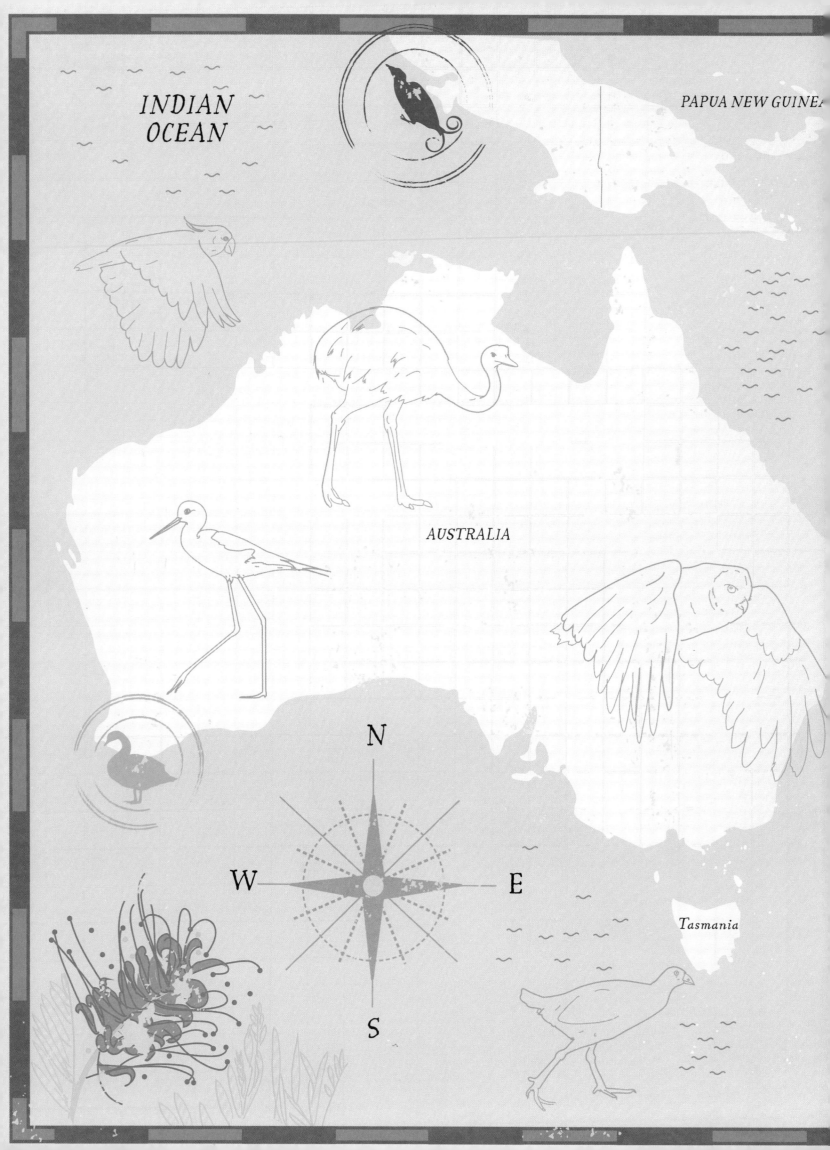

INDIAN
OCEAN

PAPUA NEW GUINEA

AUSTRALIA

N

W   E

S

Tasmania

SOLOMON
ISLANDS

New
Caledonia
(FRANCE)

TASMAN
SEA

Oceania

Oceania is a geographic area that covers a huge area of the Pacific Ocean. Its largest island by far is the continent of Australia, but Oceania also contains over 20,000 smaller islands. Many of these are uninhabited by people—making them a perfect haven for birds. However, the spread of humans over the centuries has introduced invasive species to some of these islands, sadly threatening their native wildlife. Numerous conservation efforts are under way across the continent to protect the region's native species and ensure they face a safe future.

NEW
ZEALAND

Southern cassowary
Casuarius casuarius

With its featherless neck and horned head crest, this flightless bird almost looks like a dinosaur. Although it is usually shy, it can seriously injure a person with its powerful kick and the long, bladelike claw on its inner toe. For this reason it is widely regarded as the most dangerous bird on the planet.

The cassowary is the second heaviest bird in the world after the ostrich. It weighs around 130 lb (59 kg).

The hornlike helmet, or "casque," is for pushing through thick vegetation.

6.2 ft (1.9 m) tall

The cassowary's deep call is the lowest noise of any bird and almost too deep for humans to hear!

Fleshy wattle

Cassowary eggs are bright green and bigger than a tennis ball.

Lethal claw

Chicks will stay with their father for around a year.

5.5 in. (14 cm)

Males incubate the eggs, never leaving the nest, even to eat or drink. They raise the chicks on their own.

North Island brown kiwi

Apteryx mantelli

Before humans arrived in New Zealand, its islands were dominated by birds, and the only mammals there were bats and seals. With no threat from predators, many birds lost the ability to fly, including the kiwi. Sadly, this nocturnal bird now has numerous predators, so it rarely ventures from its burrow.

The kiwi has a rather bad temper. It will charge at an attacker if it feels threatened!

In proportion to its body size, the kiwi lays the largest egg of any bird.

KEE WEE

The wings are only 1.5 in. (4 cm) long and hidden by feathers.

Threatened

There are five species of kiwi. All are classified as threatened or at risk.

Kiwis are the only birds with nostrils at the tip of their beaks— handy for sniffing out insects!

Powerful legs and large feet for running and walking

Beetles

Laughing kookaburra

Dacelo novaeguineae

High in the trees, these squat brown birds sit screeching with laughter—it is the unmistakable cackling of the laughing kookaburra. This bird is the largest member of the kingfisher family, but unlike its cousins, it doesn't feed on fish. Instead, it lives on a meaty diet of insects, lizards, and even venomous snakes.

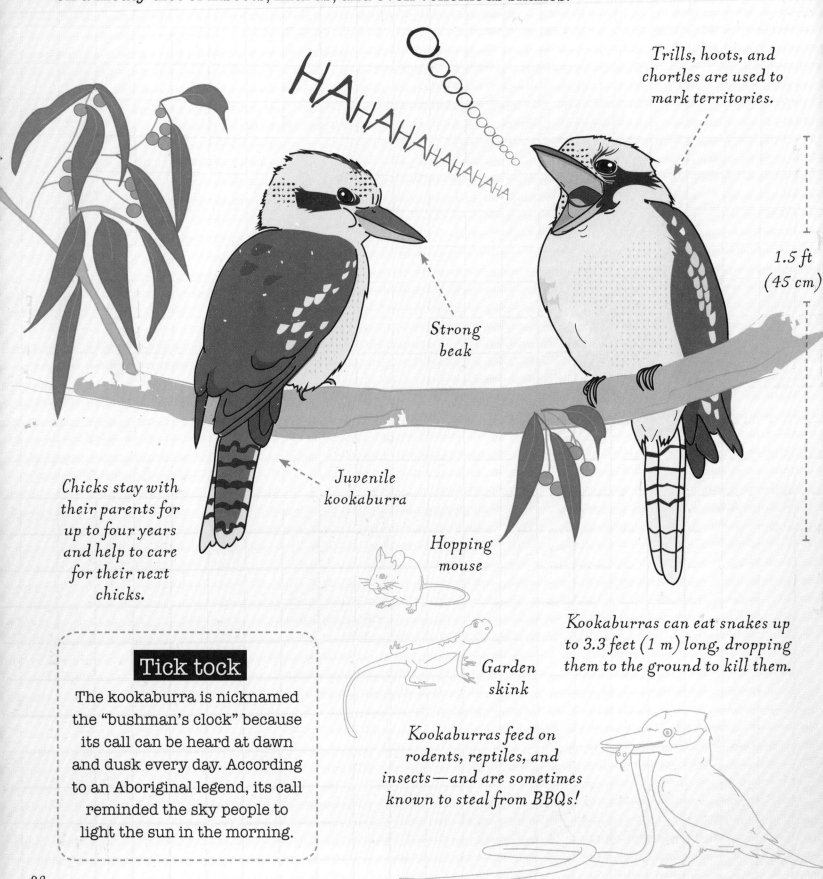

HAHAHAHAHAHAHA Oooooooo

Trills, hoots, and chortles are used to mark territories.

1.5 ft (45 cm)

Strong beak

Chicks stay with their parents for up to four years and help to care for their next chicks.

Juvenile kookaburra

Hopping mouse

Garden skink

Kookaburras can eat snakes up to 3.3 feet (1 m) long, dropping them to the ground to kill them.

Kookaburras feed on rodents, reptiles, and insects—and are sometimes known to steal from BBQs!

Tick tock

The kookaburra is nicknamed the "bushman's clock" because its call can be heard at dawn and dusk every day. According to an Aboriginal legend, its call reminded the sky people to light the sun in the morning.

Eclectus parrot

Eclectus roratus

Side-by-side, these parrots don't look alike, and for many years their contrasting colors tricked scientists into thinking they were two separate species. But in fact, they are just a male and female eclectus parrot—the female with red plumage and a black beak, and the male with bright green coloring and an orange bill.

Birds stay together for one season, then find a new mate the following year.

Broad, short bill

Male

Female

♥ *They love pandanus, a fruit found in Australia.*

The sociable birds roost in groups of up to 80.

Who's a pretty boy?

In captivity, eclectus parrots can mimic human speech, and some have impressively large vocabularies!

Females will fiercely defend the tree chosen for the couple's nest hollow.

Greater bird-of-paradise
Paradisaea apoda

Found across the islands of New Guinea, birds-of-paradise are known for their long, luscious feathers and bizarre courtship displays. The greater bird-of-paradise is the largest of them all, with a body about the size of a crow's. Its sweeping flank feathers and tail wires make it appear much larger and can be one and a half times the bird's entire body length.

To begin the courtship dance, the male raises his wings and throws his plumes over his back.

Yellow flank feathers

Wauk wauk wauk wauk

Twin tail wires

Females are brown all over to keep them camouflaged when they nest.

What's in a name?

Paradisaea apoda means "legless bird-of-paradise" because the first birds-of-paradise to arrive in Europe had been stuffed without their wings or legs. Scientists thought the birds flew using just their tail feathers and never landed!

Superb lyrebird

Menura novaehollandiae

Lyrebirds have the uncanny ability to mimic almost any sound in the forest, from the songs of other birds to human sounds like chainsaws and car alarms. Males use these noises to catch the attention of passing females, then sweep their shimmering feathers behind them in a show that's sure to impress.

Lyre-shaped outer feathers take up to eight years to grow.

Lyrebirds are named after a harplike instrument called the lyre because their curling tail resembles this shape.

12 lacelike feathers

click click

wurr

beep beep beep

whistle **wh**istle

burr burr

Lyrebirds can imitate the calls of over 20 bird species, as well as ringing phones, jackhammers, and even whistling workmen.

The male uses his long claws to scrape clear a "stage," where he will perform his display for his mate.

Fairywrens
Maluridae

These delicate birds are a popular garden visitor, but they are not as angelic as their name suggests, viciously fighting off any rivals. Despite their name, they are not members of the wren family.

Oval domed nest

Males present females with petals during courtship.

Superb fairywren
Malurus cyaneus

This bright blue bird is brown for much of the year, until males molt ahead of the mating season.

Superb fairywrens live in family groups. Non-breeding birds help to raise the young.

Females are brown all year.

Electric blue male

These territorial birds use their song to ward off rivals.

Splendid fairywren
Malurus splendens

When it is looking to attract a mate, the male's plumage turns electric blue, helping it stand out in even the remotest places, like arid scrublands and deserts.

What's the code?
Female fairywrens teach their unborn chicks a secret "password note." When the chicks hatch, they use the note to identify themselves when asking for food.

Flame bowerbird

Sericulus aureus

Bowerbirds are named after the elaborate bowers of woven sticks built by males, which they carefully "decorate" with flowers or snail shells—all there to lure a mate. The moment a female stops by, the male leaps into his courtship dance in a whirl of red and golden feathers.

The male's pupils appear larger as they dilate.

Some species decorate their bowers with pieces of plastic.

Bowers are built in the rough shape of a tunnel. Some can be up to 5 feet (1.5 m) long.

Gift

The courtship dance involves swishing the wings back and forth rapidly.

Courtship dancing: step by step

Once the female enters the bower, the male's pupils dilate, he makes a wheezing call, and then he dances, swishing his wings around him. Finally he presents the female with a gift, then ends by headbutting her!

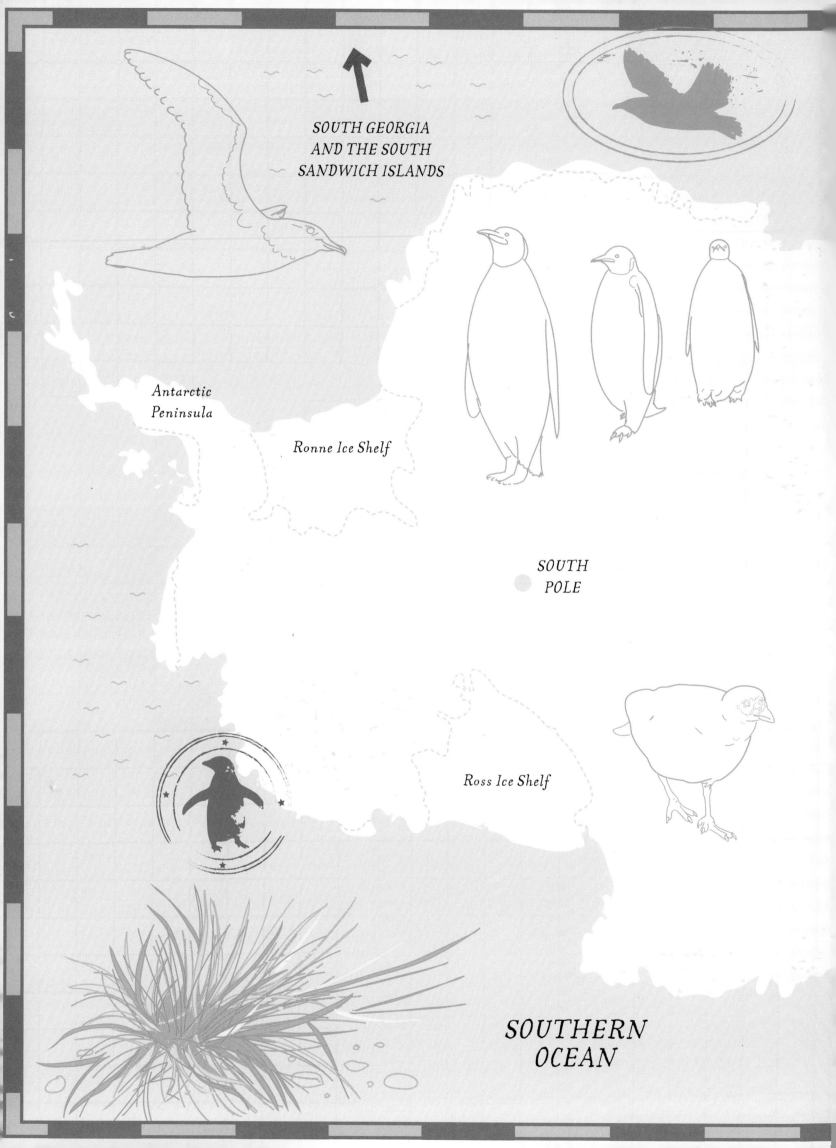

SOUTH GEORGIA
AND THE SOUTH
SANDWICH ISLANDS

Antarctic
Peninsula

Ronne Ice Shelf

SOUTH
POLE

Ross Ice Shelf

SOUTHERN
OCEAN

Amery Ice Shelf

Antarctica

Situated at the southern tip of the world, this icy continent is the coldest place on Earth, with temperatures as low as -130°F (-90°C). Around 99 percent of its mass is covered in sheet ice over 3,280 feet (1 km) thick, containing almost 70 percent of the world's fresh water. However, Antarctica's low rainfall also makes it the driest place in the world. These conditions present extraordinary challenges for the region's wildlife. The continent is uninhabited by humans (except for a handful of scientists) but is home to an array of birdlife, including soaring seabirds and crowds of huddling penguins.

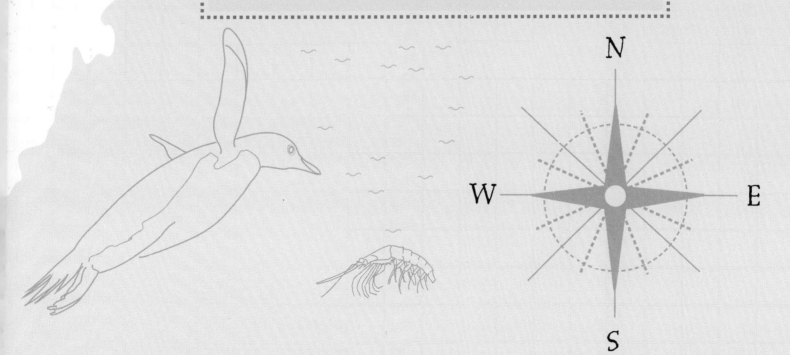

N

W   E

S

Penguins
Spheniscidae

These flightless birds are awkward on land but elegant underwater, outswimming predators such as the ferocious leopard seal. Found only in the Southern Hemisphere, they inhabit some of the planet's harshest environments, braving temperatures as low as -76°F (-60°C). But while many species live across Antarctica, others prefer a warmer climate further toward the equator.

Yellow ear patches

Antarctic temperatures drop to -76°F (-60°C) with winds of up to 124 mph (200 km/h).

0

-76

Emperor penguin
Aptenodytes forsteri

Emperors are the tallest of all penguins and the only species to breed in the Antarctic winter. After laying a single egg, females leave their breeding grounds and walk up to 21 miles (35 km) to the sea to feed. Until they return, the males care for their eggs, balancing them on their feet for around two months.

4 ft (1.2 m)

The egg is kept under a brood patch, a patch of skin that helps keep the egg warm.

Layers of feathers trap air, helping penguins stay warm. In extreme cold weather, they also huddle together for warmth.

Emperor chick

Red eyes

Pairs lay two eggs,
of which just one will
usually hatch.

Yellow crest
of feathers

Macaroni penguin

Eudyptes chrysolophus

Easily distinguished by their jaunty crest
of yellow feathers, macaroni penguins
are named after the lavish hairstyles
worn by eighteenth-century men called
macaronis. Every year, the birds spend six
months fishing at sea before building their
nests on rocky subantarctic islands.

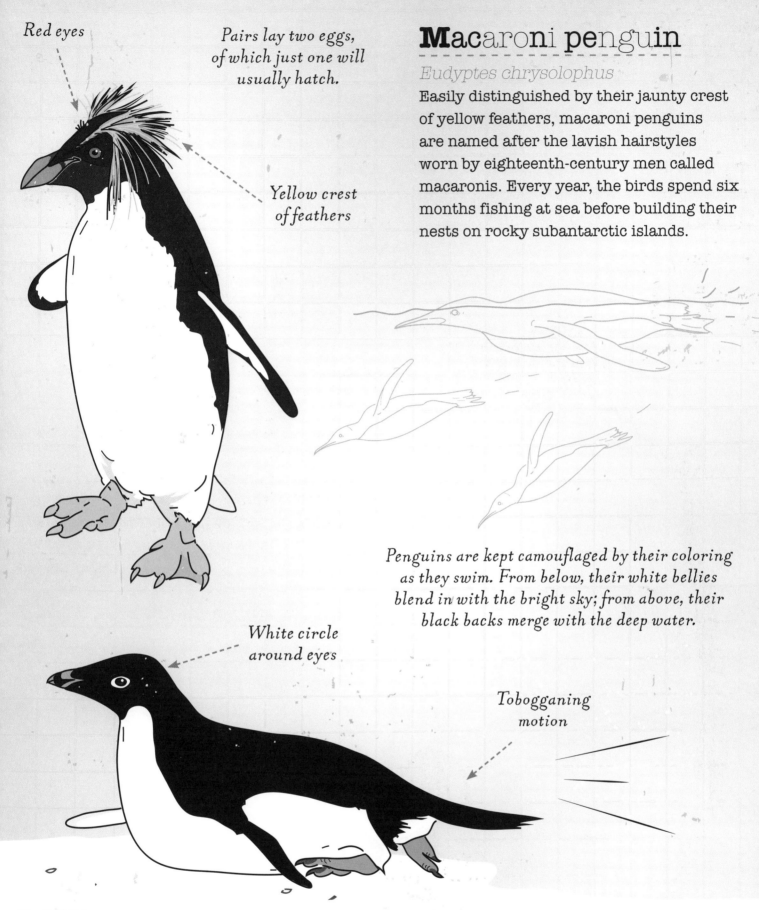

*Penguins are kept camouflaged by their coloring
as they swim. From below, their white bellies
blend in with the bright sky; from above, their
black backs merge with the deep water.*

White circle
around eyes

*Tobogganing
motion*

Adélie penguin

Pygoscelis adeliae

These cheeky midsize penguins nest in noisy groups at
rookeries along the coasts and islands of Antarctica. They make
their nests from piles of rocks and pebbles, and the naughty
penguins will often steal stones from other nearby nests!

*Adélies can travel long
distances in search of food,
often "tobogganing" across
the ice on their bellies.*

Wandering **alb**atross

Diomedea exulans

The wandering albatross has the biggest wingspan of any bird in the world, allowing it to soar on air currents for hours at a time without ever needing to flap its wings. It also has an amazing sense of smell and can follow a scent for up to 9 miles (15 km) to lead it to a fishy supper.

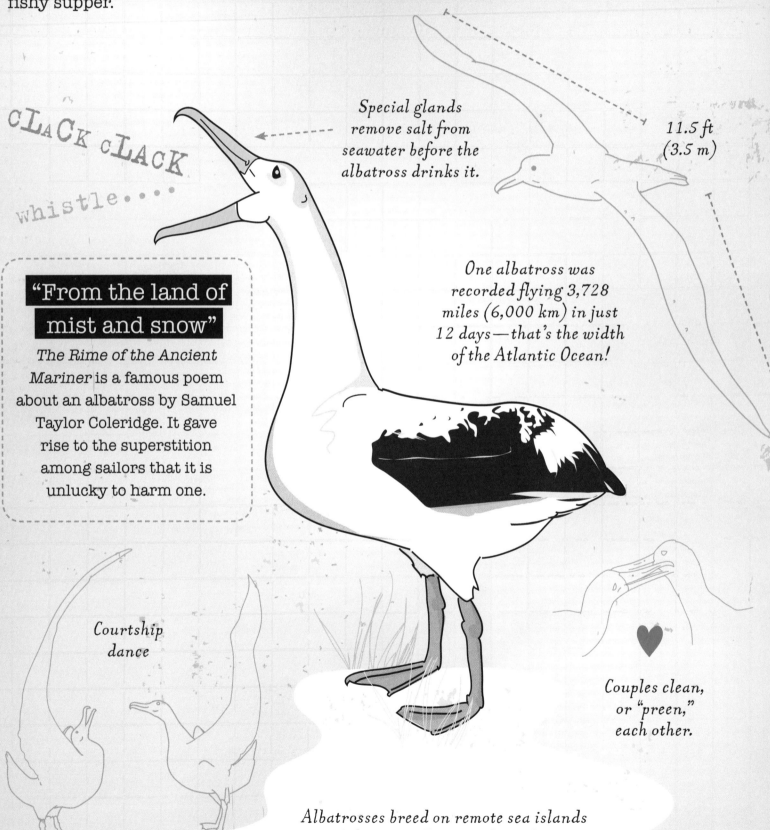

CLACK CLACK

whistle....

Special glands remove salt from seawater before the albatross drinks it.

11.5 ft (3.5 m)

"From the land of mist and snow"

The Rime of the Ancient Mariner is a famous poem about an albatross by Samuel Taylor Coleridge. It gave rise to the superstition among sailors that it is unlucky to harm one.

One albatross was recorded flying 3,728 miles (6,000 km) in just 12 days—that's the width of the Atlantic Ocean!

Courtship dance

Couples clean, or "preen," each other.

Albatrosses breed on remote sea islands every other year. Pairs perform elaborate courtship rituals and mate for life.

Arctic tern

Sterna paradisaea

Every year, the Arctic tern undertakes an epic migration, traveling nearly from pole to pole—a round-trip journey of up to 50,000 miles (96,000 km), the longest animal migration in the world. They spend summer breeding in the Northern Hemisphere, but before winter they fly south to Antarctica, where summer is just starting. This means they may never witness a winter!

Terns can dive at up to 31 mph (50 km/h) to catch fish.

Long tail streamers mean the Arctic tern is sometimes nicknamed the "sea swallow."

Black cap of feathers

Before taking flight, flocks grow completely silent—a moment referred to as "the dread."

The beak and feet turn from black to red in breeding season.

Travel routes of an Arctic tern

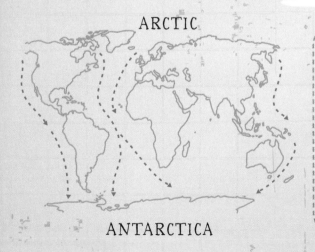

ARCTIC

ANTARCTICA

Fly me to the Moon

Arctic terns live for up to 30 years. During their lifetime, they may travel up to 1,670,000 miles (2,700,000 km). That's the equivalent of flying to the Moon and back three times!

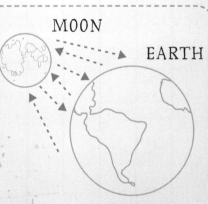

MOON

EARTH

Index